More Math, Please!

Kid-Friendly Computation

★ ★ ★ Level 2, Numbers over 10 ★ ★ ★

SARAH PERRY MORGAN

Zephyr Press

Tucson, Arizona

About Zephyr Press

Founded in 1979 in Tucson, Arizona, Zephyr Press continually strives to provide quality, innovative products for our customers, with the goal of improving learning opportunities for all children. With a focus on gifted education, multiple intelligences, and brain-compatible learning, Zephyr Press material is selected to help *all* children reach their highest potential.

More Math, Please! Kid-Friendly Computation—Level 2, Numbers over 10
© 2002 by Sarah Perry Morgan

Grades: PreK–3

Printed in the United States of America

ISBN: 1-56976-140-X

Editing: Kirsteen E. Anderson
Design and Production: Dan Miedaner
Illustrations: Sarah Perry Morgan
Cover: Dan Miedaner

Published by:
Zephyr Press
P.O. Box 66006
Tucson, Arizona 85728-6006
800-232-2187
www.zephyrpress.com
www.i-home-school.com

≥ Zephyr Press is a registered trademark of Zephyr Press, Inc.

Library of Congress Cataloging-in-Publication Data

Morgan, Sarah (Sarah K.) 1953–
    More math, please! : kid-friendly computation, level 2: numbers over 10 / Sarah Morgan.
       p. cm
    Includes bibliographical references and index.
    ISBN 1-56976-140-X (alk. paper)
      1. Mathematics—Study and teaching (Elementary) 2. Addition. 3. Subtraction. I. Title.
QA135.6 .M68 2001
372.7'2—dc21   2001046627

For my darlings, Matthew and Melissa,
who always believe in me.

Contents

How to Use This Book

The following table outlines the contents of this book, with a brief explanation of the focus of each chapter.

Chapter	Content
Chapter 1: *How Children Learn*	**Who is targeted and why:** Identifying the children who have difficulty with math and ways to address this difficulty.
Chapter 2: *Reviewing Prerequisite Skills*	**Prior knowledge:** Identifying students' background knowledge and reviewing foundational concepts before moving into multi-digit computation.
Chapter 3: *Place Value*	**Teaching place value to young ones:** Presenting a hands-on, whole-body method of teaching place value that draws on real-world applications.
Chapter 4: *Computation Using Place-Value Mats*	**Practicing place value on mats:** Using real materials as a class or in small groups to gain fluency in understanding and using place value.
Chapter 5: *A Bird's-Eye View*	**Looking globally at all problems through 20:** Identifying problems and their place within the global whole of computation; working with problems children already know.
Chapter 6: *Make a Ten*	**Learning a method of addition to 20 based on place value:** Working with addition problems that require making a ten, using real materials and building on prior knowledge.
Chapter 7: *Take from Ten*	**Learning a method of subtraction from 20 based on place value:** Working with subtraction problems that require taking a ten, using real materials and building on prior knowledge.
Chapter 8: *Taking Stock*	**Assessing fluency with new concepts:** Reviewing thoroughly all newly learned material to check for mastery.
Chapter 9: *To the Top!*	**Extending the method for all multi-digit numbers:** Using this method for all numbers, for those students who want to learn more.

Preparation for Using This Book

Before beginning this book, familiarize yourself with the elements of good practice discussed in chapters 2 ("Good Practices") and 3 ("Assessment Practices That Work") of *More Math, Please!—Level 1* (hereafter referred to as book 1). These elements drive the method in this book as well. Also review the concepts of visual imprinting and visual connections discussed in chapter 4 of book 1 ("Learning Numbers"). You should also be fluent with the fives-frames, "my two hands," and the Stony Brook Village houses for math facts to ten.

Deciding Where to Start

For students just finishing book 1: Skip right to chapter 3 and begin the new material.

For students who finished book 1 but have had an extended break: Begin with chapter 2 to review and brush up the students' skills in preparation for the new material.

For students brand-new to the *More Math, Please!* method: Students will need to be fluent with the contents of book 1, chapters 4–7. Much of this information is reviewed in chapter 2 of this book, but for students who need additional practice, work through part II of book 1, then begin with chapter 3 of this book and proceed from there.

For students needing remediation: Determine whether the students have weaknesses in computation using numbers to ten. If they do, use chapter 2 of this book extensively to teach the fundamentals before attempting multi-digit computation. If necessary, work through book 1, chapters 5–7 at the students' pace before introducing chapter 3 of this book and proceeding from there.

Introduction

My own struggles with math during my elementary years fueled my passion to discover ways of teaching that would result in success for all students. I grew up saying and believing that I just "didn't have a mathematical mind." I've since learned that my strongly visual view of the world is a great enhancement to the understanding of math, if I utilize my visual mind in the learning and doing of math.

In graduate school, I experienced full-blown panic when I had to take my math methods class. The only way I could make sense of the problems was to draw pictures of what was going on in them. My panic skyrocketed the night my professor leaned over where I sat hunched, trying to hide the little pictures I was drawing. In spite of my best attempts to cover my paper with both arms, her sharp eyes spied the drawings and she snatched my paper up. Waving it in the air, she bellowed, "Look at what Sarah's doing!" My mortification was complete. My body felt chilled, but my face burned and my stomach clenched so tightly I thought I would be sick.

What happened next surprised me. The professor went on to say that the ability to visualize math and to draw pictures of what was happening would make me a good teacher, because most children are very visual and learn better with the use of visuals. She took what to me had always been an embarrassment and pronounced it good. I will never forget that night!

During the past several years, I have worked closely with a wide variety of learners, struggling mightily to understand what they needed in order to learn efficiently. I made it my mission to figure out the ways children learn best by throwing out any procedure that did not work for all of the students or that shut them down, did not hold their interest, or intimidated them in any way. Over time, I learned that there are some basic elements of good practice that work with all my students regardless of their individual learning styles.

The methods in the *More Math, Please!* series are the result of eight years of working with children while focusing on the question, "What makes it possible for all of them to learn?" This quest intensified as I worked on my graduate studies in education. At the same time as I was working through content and learning challenges in my "lab" with the children, I was reading about the same learning issues in my classes. The result for me was maximized understanding. It is this understanding I want to share with you, in the hope that something in this series will energize your teaching and help you give all your students the experience of success.

I am grateful to the people who together supported this work: my own children, who cheered me on; my students' parents, who believed in me *and* in their own children; and the professors who let me concentrate on the topics that really interested me. To the darling students I have worked with, all I can say is, "Thanks for letting me learn from you! You are the best!"

Chapter 1
How Children Learn

To fully understand the value of this method of teaching computation, it is important to take the time to look globally at learning styles and how they relate to traditional ways of teaching math. This overview will lead naturally into identifying the factors that are necessary for a math method to be successful for all children, regardless of their learning needs.

The whole topic of teaching to multiple learning styles can be very intimidating to overworked teachers and parents. Because this is true, I first provide an orientation to the learning needs children have, and then pull all the ideas together and draw some conclusions that will help to bring the seemingly disparate elements together into a simple plan for good teaching practice.

The chart on page 3 presents an overview of the learning styles that I consider critical to this discussion. (For in-depth information on these and other learning styles, please refer to Barbe 1985; Gardner 1993; Gregorc 1982; Tobias 1994; and Witkin 1977.) If we imagine that the learning styles on the right side of the chart represent real children in real classrooms, it will become easier to see which children are being "taught around" in traditional methods of teaching.

Learning Styles in Traditional Methods of Teaching Math

Math is normally taught in tiny steps; students are given seemingly unrelated bits of information to work with or are given steps to memorize for solving problems, typically without any explanation of *why* those steps work. Often there is no real-life application within the problems, and all too often, students work solely with paper and pencil, having no opportunity to construct meaning for themselves using real objects.

Is it possible to teach math, as seemingly concrete and sequential as it is, in a way that will reach the abstract, random, visual/spatial, kinesthetic, and global students? Or should we continue trying to force them over to the left side of the chart? It seems more reasonable to change our current practice to fit the children rather than trying to force children to be something they cannot be. Let's make the assumption, then, that we should expand our method of teaching math to encompass and embrace all our students. What we will do in this book is approach computation in a global, visual, kinesthetic, abstract, and random way so that no child is left out!

The Common Denominator

I have come to believe that children who are highly visual also tend to be global, somewhat random, and kinesthetic. Think about it. Visual children see a whole picture, see smaller elements within their own environment, see their connection to other elements in the whole picture, and tend to remember parts of the picture based on where each part fits into the whole. In addition, highly visual children will move randomly through the picture (or map or pattern) and are often inclined to spatial activities that require physical skill. Visual children will prefer to see the task done as they learn it, rather than hearing it explained, and will profit from doing the problem themselves. It is important for these children to understand *why* the formula works by seeing how one action affects other parts within the whole. They might not understand the process the way another student does, but if they are certain of the goal of the lesson, they will likely invent good steps that make sense to them and allow them to reach the goal.

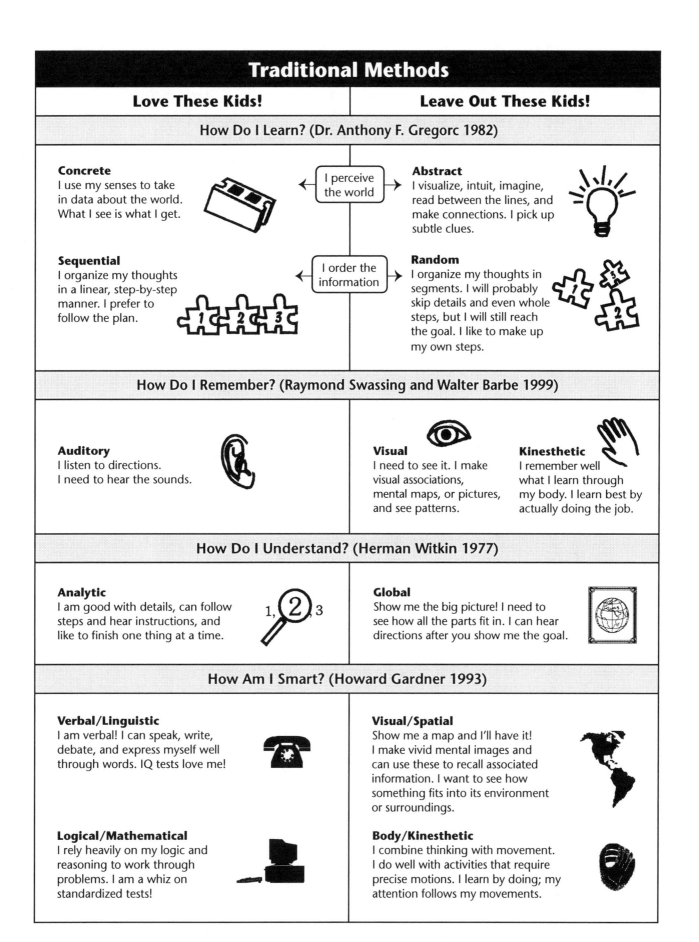

Traditional Methods

Love These Kids!	Leave Out These Kids!

How Do I Learn? (Dr. Anthony F. Gregorc 1982)

Concrete
I use my senses to take in data about the world. What I see is what I get.

I perceive the world

Abstract
I visualize, intuit, imagine, read between the lines, and make connections. I pick up subtle clues.

Sequential
I organize my thoughts in a linear, step-by-step manner. I prefer to follow the plan.

I order the information

Random
I organize my thoughts in segments. I will probably skip details and even whole steps, but I will still reach the goal. I like to make up my own steps.

How Do I Remember? (Raymond Swassing and Walter Barbe 1999)

Auditory
I listen to directions. I need to hear the sounds.

Visual
I need to see it. I make visual associations, mental maps, or pictures, and see patterns.

Kinesthetic
I remember well what I learn through my body. I learn best by actually doing the job.

How Do I Understand? (Herman Witkin 1977)

Analytic
I am good with details, can follow steps and hear instructions, and like to finish one thing at a time.

1, 2, 3

Global
Show me the big picture! I need to see how all the parts fit in. I can hear directions after you show me the goal.

How Am I Smart? (Howard Gardner 1993)

Verbal/Linguistic
I am verbal! I can speak, write, debate, and express myself well through words. IQ tests love me!

Visual/Spatial
Show me a map and I'll have it! I make vivid mental images and can use these to recall associated information. I want to see how something fits into its environment or surroundings.

Logical/Mathematical
I rely heavily on my logic and reasoning to work through problems. I am a whiz on standardized tests!

Body/Kinesthetic
I combine thinking with movement. I do well with activities that require precise motions. I learn by doing; my attention follows my movements.

Unique Features of the *More Math, Please!* Method

1. Students are able to add and subtract multi-digit numbers using the same strategies they learned in book 1 for computing to ten, including "my two hands." For this reason, I studiously avoid terms such as *borrowing* or *carrying*. Every step I do is based on adding numbers under ten or subtracting numbers from ten. Carefully limiting the procedures to these basic facts ensures students will be successful in computation with numbers of any size.

2. A critical feature is that rote memorization—whether of answers to problems, steps in solving a problem, or procedures for computation—is avoided at all costs. Memorization is not the answer. Drill and repetition of facts might result in short-term memorization for some students, but not for every one. If you take the time to tie a process, a fact, or a procedure to a story, long-term recall is much more likely because the procedure is tied to something else that acts as a trigger for recall.

3. In this book, the actions of adding and subtracting are tied directly to stories from the beginning, so that students are able to "see" computation taking place. As a result, they not only understand and remember what is going on, they also can easily determine which action to use when they are presented with story problems.

4. Computation is introduced using concrete materials in order to add a visual component, which is a huge aid for learning. Having children do the actions of computation using real materials will also cement the procedures in their minds.

5. Part of the reason for the great success of the methods in the *More Math, Please!* series is due to the fact that they tap auditory, kinesthetic/ tactile, and visual components simultaneously. Whatever I teach, I teach to the ears, eyes, and hands. "See, say, and do" is the rule of thumb.

6. Assessments are an important component of this program. My philosophy on assessments is radically different from the traditional one. I believe that the purpose of teaching is to provide all children with the opportunity to master the material and that all children are capable of mastery. Assessments are simply activities that reflect back to us as teachers the success or failure of our own teaching. My assessments are often reproductions of worksheets the children have done during daily lessons. My assessments simply measure whether the children indeed know the material I have taught them. There is no point, then, in presenting the material in a different format. The children either will or will not know how to do the computation. I often

recommend giving a second assessment in order to rule out the possibility that a child who did not do well was simply tired, distracted, or having an "off" day.

7. If a child is unable to correctly complete a portion of the material in an assessment, this is a signal that reteaching needs to occur. Assessments are tools for determining mastery and areas needing reteaching, *not* means by which to level or sort students. The subtle shift in our thinking as teachers, from "grading kids," to leading them to complete mastery of the material, leads to incredible gains in learning. All our students are likely to become fluent and competent with the required work.

8. I allow, even encourage, students to retake the same test after more practice if they are not satisfied with their performance. I began doing so because many of the children I teach have failed so often that they have given up trying or believing in their ability to learn. The results were unexpected, however. I've had students ask to retake a test not because they didn't pass, but because they wanted to feel more confident with the material. Recently, after scoring 100 percent on their test in my classroom, my fourth graders decided to retake the test in their regular classrooms "just for fun." I'm not kidding; those were their words. Allowing retakes not only increases mastery, it (a) increases confidence, (b) raises the students' expectations of themselves, from simply passing to becoming fluent and confident with the material, and (c) encourages students to take ownership of their own learning.

Putting It All Together

Now let's take these ideas and distill from them some basic elements of a good teaching approach that will engage children from both sides of the learning styles chart:

1. State the goal first. Explain what the children are going to learn and why it is important. What is the point, the bottom line?

2. Provide concrete materials to the children and establish clear but general parameters within which they will work. Then let them manipulate the materials until they can see the action that occurs in a computation and how that action affects the whole.

3. Communicate with the students about what they have discovered and guide them in drawing conclusions. This step involves pattern detection and exploration. It will be through patterns that they recall specific facts.

4. Present real-life examples of using these sums. Use stories whenever you possibly can. Stories help demonstrate to students how math is relevant. They help answer the inevitable question, "When am I ever going to need to know this?"

5. Allow as much practice in solving problems as the students need.

6. Don't expect the students to "just remember" anything. Instead, tie every new concept to a previously learned concept, using visual and movement cues.

7. Develop a habit of teaching to all three modalities.

Chapter 2
Reviewing Prerequisite Skills

Goals for This Chapter

1. To review the meaning of numbers
2. To review the relationships between numbers
3. To review the "my two hands" computation strategy
4. To review dot cards and fives frames
5. To review the number houses to ten

It is critical to approach the lessons in this book only after reviewing previously learned skills. Not only will the exercises ease your students into the new material gently, but they will provide you with feedback as to where each student is in the learning process. Taking ample time at the beginning to bring every child up to speed will ensure that no one starts the new book already feeling left behind!

The main headings in this chapter correspond to the areas of prior knowledge needed for multi-digit computation. Under each heading are suggested activities. Simply stated, if students have not mastered this content, the lessons in this book will not work. Each day spent in review up front will pay generous dividends in rapid learning later. Because the method in this book is based entirely upon the material in book 1, to learn multi-digit computation, your students simply will be taking those earlier skills, refining them, and applying them to new situations. For this reason, it is critical to ensure that they are fluent with these background concepts. Even if your students have studied book 1 in a prior year, a review will refresh their memories. Much can be forgotten over a summer!

The Meaning of Numbers

Begin by laying a visual background for the numbers to ten. The value of visual imprinting is discussed in depth in book 1, chapter 4. Your goal is for the children to have a visual image of the quantity each number represents. Using dots to represent the numbers is an effective way to accomplish this (see following illustration).

Discovery

Locate the dot cards (blackline master 2.1 on page 65) and photocopy them onto transparency film for use with an overhead projector. Also photocopy several sets on paper or card stock and laminate them for use in math centers.

Display the progression of dots from one to ten:

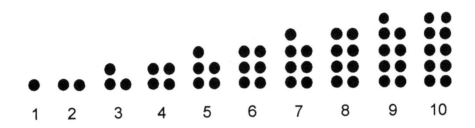

Ask the children to talk about what they notice about the numbers. Which groups of dots have similar shapes? Which numbers have an "odd fellow" on top? Discover and compare how many pairs of dots each quantity has. Identify which numbers have the same number of dot pairs (two and three, four and five, and so on). Ask questions such as these: How many odd numbers are there? How many even? Why do you suppose that is? How many numbers have a four-dot pattern in them? Are there any numbers made solely of three-dot patterns?

Number-Recognition Activities

Use the laminated dot cards for a variety of card games, which children can play independently in the math center.

War: Students play in pairs. Each player lays down a card simultaneously. In the traditional game, the player who lays down the higher number gets both cards. The child has to correctly name both quantities laid down in order to take the cards (without counting dots!). For variations, have the lower quantity win, or odd over even, and so on.

Memory: A small group can play memory using two sets of cards. Again, the children should name the quantities they turn over without counting the dots.

Go fish: Using four sets of cards for a small group, have children play go fish. Each player has to ask for the desired card by name, not by showing the card to the group.

Name that number: Students work together in pairs, using the dot cards as flash cards. One child holds up a card and the other names it as quickly as possible. Have students trade off roles of holding up and naming cards.

Relationships between Numbers

For number relationships, begin with the fives-frame number chart (see blackline master 2.2 on page 66). You can photocopy enough copies for each child to have one, or project one copy on an overhead projector. You may wish to laminate for durability.

Begin by displaying a filled-in number chart for group discovery time. Ask the children to talk about the patterns they see. Where and how do numbers repeat? Find numeral patterns such as 1, 6, 1, 6, 1 and 2, 7, 2, 7, 2 and 3, 8, 3, 8, 3, and so forth. Examine the fives column and notice how the numbers in the tens position repeat (10, 15, 20, 25, 30, 35, 40, 45, etc.). What is significant about this pattern?

Children who are highly visual will recognize additional patterns as they continue to use this chart. For example, they might note that adding five to any number yields the number directly underneath it on the chart. If they add ten, they will skip down two rows. If they add four, they will skip down one row then move one space to the left. To add six, they move down one row then move one space to the right. Chess players may relate these movements on the fives-frame chart to the moves of chess pieces.

1	2	3	4	5
6	7	8	9	10
11	12	13	14	15
16	17	18	19	20
21	22	23	24	25
26	27	28	29	30
31	32	33	34	35
36	37	38	39	40
41	42	43	44	45
46	47	48	49	50
51	52	53	54	55
56	57	58	59	60
61	62	63	64	65
66	67	68	69	70
71	72	73	74	75

Number-Recognition Activities

Full frame: Give each child a blank fives-frame chart to 20 (blackline master 2.3, page 67). Call out numbers at random, asking students to write each number in the box where it belongs. This activity is self-assessing, because when you are finished, the children can check their own work to see if their numbers appear in the correct sequence.

Fives-frame patterns: Again using the blank fives-frame chart in blackline master 2.3, call out questions that require children to recognize the patterns within the chart. For example, "Write the number under eight" or "Write the number above six." This activity will help cement in students' minds the relationships between the numbers in each column of the chart.

How high can you go?: Make numerous copies of the long blank fives-frame chart in blackline master 2.4 (page 68) and cut apart along the dotted line. Give each child several charts to tape together end-to-end to form a *really* long chart. (Each child can choose how long to make his or her chart.) Then, the children write in all the numbers to fill their charts.

Fives-Frame Dot Cards

Use the fives-frame dot cards (blackline masters 2.5a–b, pages 69–70) to help children visualize where each number falls in relationship to the base of ten. The number at the end of each full row (here, 5, 10, 15, 20) becomes an "anchor number" to which numbers are added or subtracted to yield quantities in partial rows. This visual imprinting allows children to see computation globally, a particular benefit to those who are not logical-sequential thinkers. You can also use the cards to practice oral computation. Have the student begin by naming the quantity shown (e.g., 12). Then ask questions such as, "How many more dots would you need to make 15?" "How many would you have if I gave you only two more?" "What about if I took away four?" Students can also play the card games listed on pages 8–9, such as go fish or memory.

Visual Imprinting for Computation

Give each student a copy of blackline master 2.1, the dot cards, and some colored pencils. Using the dot card transparencies you made for the "Meaning of Numbers" activities, place one card at a time on the overhead. Guide students to recognize subgroups within each dot pattern. Let's use these dot cards as an example to illustrate the process:

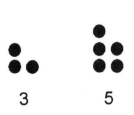

For the three-dot pattern: Ask students to find 2 + 1 in this dot pattern. Have them circle the two dots and one dot separately using their colored pencils.

For the five-dot pattern: Ask whether students can find a 4 + 1 pattern in this dot grouping. Have them circle the four dots and one dot separately. Now have them look for a 2 + 3 grouping. Using a different color, have them circle the two dots and three dots separately.

Continue in this manner with each set of dots until students have circled all the possible number combinations that add up to each number from two to ten. I have also provided sheets of hollow dots (see blackline masters 2.6a–b, pages 71–72). If you would prefer, you can have children color in the subsets of dots with their colored pencils, rather than circling them. These pages can be stapled together to make a number book for each child.

My Two Hands

Now show each dot card again. As you identify the subgroupings this time, have the children show you the computation on their hands. The "my two hands" strategy is explained in detail in chapter 6 of book 1. In brief, it is a kinesthetic and visual method of showing computations by spreading the fingers apart or moving them together. Two is represented with the index and middle fingers, four with all four fingers, five with the fingers and thumb, six with the fingers and thumb of one hand plus the thumb of the other, and so on. To add any pair of numbers totaling up to ten, students can represent each number on their fingers and simultaneously see the sum. The following illustration shows the sums for five:

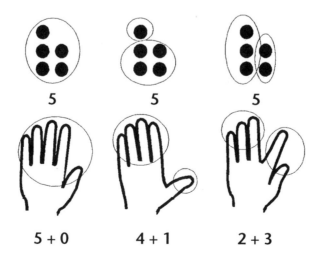

Number Houses to Ten

Using blackline masters 2.7–2.21 (pages 73–87), follow these steps to ensure children have mastered computations to ten. For any child who struggles with the number-house activities, back up and provide plenty of practice with the earlier activities before reintroducing number houses.

1. Refer to chapter 7 of book 1, if necessary, to explain the rules for filling in the houses.

2. Give each student a set of concrete objects, such as plastic counters. Have the students count out three counters, then figure out how many ways they can group them ($3 + 0$ and $1 + 2$).

3. When students have discovered the possible groupings for three, give them the "Figure out which families can live in each house" blackline master for threes (2.7a, page 73) and have them write in the number combinations they discovered with their chips.

4. Next present the trifold blackline master of blank houses for Third Street (blackline master 2.8, which has two houses in each row). Have them fold under the bottom two sections, then fill in the top two houses with the correct numbers. (Each attic will have the numeral 3 in it, and the two floors will show the combinations that make up three, namely the numerals 0 and 3 in the first house and 1 and 2 in the second.) When finished, they fold that section down and show the second row of houses. They complete that row in the same way, then turn to the last row of houses (thus practicing the same sums three times).

5. Repeat steps 2 through 4 for the number four (using blackline master 2.7b for "Figure out which families can live in each house" and blackline master 2.9 for practice houses).

6. Next, give students the page of mixed addition and subtraction problems for three and four to complete (see blackline master 2.10, page 76).

7. Repeat steps 2–6 for the numbers five and six (using blackline masters 2.9, 2.11a–b, 2.12, and 2.13). There is also a worksheet that mixes problems for sums from three to six (blackline master 2.14, page 80). Then repeat the process for the numbers seven and eight (using blackline masters 2.12, 2.15a–b, 2.16, and 2.17). Finally, repeat the process for the numbers nine and ten (using blackline masters 2.16, 2.18a–b, 2.19, 2.20, and 2.21). Note that blackline master 2.21 has a mix of problems for sums from seven to ten.

When the class can do all these problems fluently, move on to chapter 3!

Assessments

For your convenience, an individual assessment report and two whole-class record charts are provided in Appendix B on pages 203–5. They are designed for recording students' mastery of the concepts reviewed in this chapter. You can use the following assessment procedures to check for mastery of each concept. Remember that any student who has not mastered all these math skills fluently will falter as new material is introduced throughout the rest of the book. So if any students struggle, provide small-group teaching until they demonstrate readiness to move on.

Dot patterns: Mix up the set of dot card transparencies. Write down the order of the transparencies so you have an answer key to check students' papers. One at a time, show each transparency briefly. Have the children write the numeral represented by that dot pattern on their paper.

Blank fives frame to 20: Give each student a blank fives-frame chart to 20 (use blackline master 2.3, page 67). Call out each number from 1 to 20 in a random order (record the order for yourself). Have students write each number you call out in its correct location in the fives frame.

Dot flash cards: Using the fives-frame dot cards (blackline masters 2.5a and 2.5b, pages 69–70), mix them up in a random order. (Record the order for your answer key.) Flash each card briefly and have the students write down the numeral corresponding to that dot set on their papers.

Colored dot subsets: Using the pages of hollow dots (blackline masters 2.6a and 2.6b, pages 71–72), color each set of dots in two different colors to represent a pair of numbers that totals that sum (for example, five dots = 3 + 2). Hold up one of these sets of dots. Have the students represent the sum on their hands using the "my two hands" strategy.

Mixed number-house problems: Give each student a sheet (or sheets) of mixed addition and subtraction problems for all the numbers to ten.

Chapter 3
Place Value

Goals for This Chapter

1. To act out the concept of place value

2. To apply the concept of place value to real-life situations

3. To demonstrate understanding of place value using concrete materials

---

Although place value traditionally is not introduced until middle elementary grades, I teach place value early as a key element of computation with multi-digit numbers. Using the visual/kinesthetic approach of *More Math, Please!*, students will first see what place value means in concrete terms, to enable them to utilize this concept as they work through the lessons in this book. Because place value is demonstrated in concrete terms using attic numerals 1 and 10, children can embrace the concept as early as kindergarten.

Concrete Practice with Place Value

Just as simple sums were introduced using a story to place them in a real-world context, I extend the Stony Brook story to introduce the concept of place value:

> In Stony Brook Village, just over the brook from the residential area, there is a town square with office buildings all around it. Each building is new and clean and shaded by big trees. Pointed roofs crown each building, and attic numbers (1 and 10, which represent place value) are painted on the attics like this. (Show an overhead of the empty buildings; use blackline master 3.1 on page 88.)

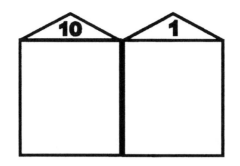

The planning commission has hired you as the property manager for one of the office buildings, and it is your job to rent office space to people who want to work inside your building. (Point to the side of the building labeled 1.) There are nine desks in this office. That means on this side you can rent desks to nine people, and no more. (Point to the side labeled 10.) On this side are big tables, each seating ten people. (**Note:** In this context the 10 and 1 represent place values, not a numerical total of the number of workers.)

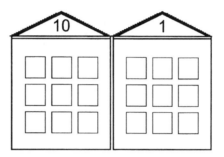

Ten people exactly—no more, no less—must sit around each table. Once you have rented all the desks on the ones side of the building, if more people come in looking for a place to work, you will need to take ten people from the ones side and move them over to a big table on the tens side. Then you can fill up the desks on the ones side again. Each time you get ten or more people on the ones side, you have to move a group of ten next door. If you don't, and you leave too many people on the ones side, the commission will hear about it, and they will come with their sirens screaming to give you a ticket!

More people wanting to come in. →

Activities for Place Value

Act it out: Use masking tape to outline on the floor the two sides of the office, large enough that ten children can actually fit inside. (Make sure the tens side is on the left, to mirror the order of the tens place and ones place in a written number.) Place nine chairs inside the ones office and leave the tens side empty. Tell a story in which you come to the office one day, unlock the door, and soon three children arrive, wanting to rent desks. Have three volunteers step forward, welcome them, and show them to their desks. Continue adding more occupants until the children tell you that you have reached the magic number of ten. Then have the class work out what to do next—don't tell them; let them talk it out. At this point introduce the phrase "make a ten," which you will use repeatedly throughout the method. Usher a group of ten next door, then take a large satin ribbon and gently tie the children together so they represent a group. They will not forget this object lesson! During the game, you want to reinforce the pattern of filling up the ones side first; then, when the side fills up, making a group of ten and moving the group of ten next door. The motion is "in and to the left," which will be mirrored in written computation.

Rent-an-office game: This is a good game for children to play in the math center. Reproduce and laminate the game cards in blackline master 3.2 (page 89). Also photocopy the place-value mats in blackline masters 3.3a–b (pages 90–91). Place the two pages of blackline master 3.3 side by side and photocopy onto 11" x 17" paper (making sure the tens side is on the left). Either a pair or small group of children can play. Give the children a handful of rubber bands and a pack of wooden craft sticks. The children take turns drawing a game card and placing the corresponding number of craft sticks ("workers seeking office space") on the ones place mat (the "office building"). As soon as the number of craft sticks exceeds nine, the children count out ten sticks, bundle them with a rubber band, and move them over to the tens place-value mat. The purpose of this game is to practice the action of bundling ("making a ten") and then moving the bundle of ten next door. Encourage children to continue playing until they are fluent with the actions of bundling and moving sticks to represent the concept of place value.

Rent-an-office cards

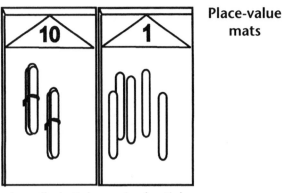

Place-value mats

bundled sticks   single sticks

The Transition from Concrete to Symbolic

When you make the transition from the renting-an-office scenario to symbols, go slowly and explain what you are doing carefully, so the students do not become confused and think you are introducing a new concept. Talk out what the children have been doing in the rent-an-office game and how these actions can be represented with numbers. I like to use the place-value mat transparency and an overhead projector, but you could also draw with chalk on a chalkboard. First model for the class the action of renting out office space and making a bundle of ten using the craft sticks. Then stop and ask, "How many tens do you have on this side?" As the children answer, write the number they say below the tens office with a wipe-off marker. Then ask, "How many ones do you have on this side?" and write that number below the ones side (see illustration).

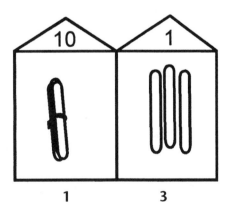

Continue adding sticks to the ones side, bundling them, and moving them over to the tens side, until you have two bundles on the tens side and some number of single sticks on the ones side. Stop again and ask, "How many tens? How many ones?," writing the numbers below the corresponding place mats.

Next show the children a set of sticks arranged on the place-value mat and ask them to write the corresponding number. Do this several times until everyone can confidently write the correct symbols for the sets.

Last of all, show the children a number and have them draw the visual representation of that number in stick format (see illustration). Blackline master 3.4 (page 92) contains a set of blank place-value cards in which children can draw sticks. Repeat this step until the students have mastered it.

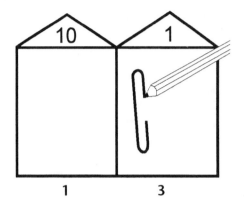

"What Is This?" Game

"What is this?" is a good activity for children to do in pairs in the math center. To prepare, duplicate the place-value cards in blackline masters 3.5a–c (pages 93–95) and laminate. These cards will have several uses in wrapping up this chapter.

Place-value cards

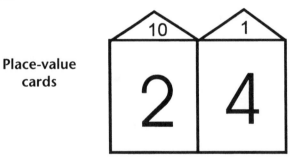

1. One child holds up a card with numbers printed in the place-value houses. The second child identifies the number in terms of how many tens and ones it contains. For example, if the first child holds up 24, the second child would say, "Two 10s and four 1s."

2. Children can duplicate the numbers using craft sticks and the place-value mats in blackline masters 3.3a–b. Each child takes a turn drawing a card, then sets out sticks to represent that number on the mat.

3. Children can take turns setting out sets of sticks on the place-value mats for their partners to identify using written numerals.

Taking It Further

Inevitably, some child will ask, "What if we keep getting more and more tens?" In this case, you may wish to introduce the 100s office and explain that only nine bundles of ten are allowed in the tens office. Thus, the tens office has the same rule as the ones office: "no more than nine." Point out that as you move left, each attic number gains one more zero. My students loved working with base ten models and filling the offices for 1s, 10s, 100s, and 1,000s. They started with the ones, bundled a ten, added nine more tens so they could bundle 100, and kept on going. I wrapped up by asking, "How many?" for each office and writing the number below the office. In this way, they could see that the zero means "there is no one in this office."

Because the children were interested, we continued the exploration of the four offices. I set up a model using craft sticks, and the children wrote the number it represented. Then I changed the model, and they changed their number to reflect the new model. There is something about really big numbers that fascinates children, and this activity makes large numbers understandable and accessible to them.

Assessments

An individual progress report and a whole-class record listing the skills covered in chapters 3 and 4 can be found in Appendix B (pages 206 and 207). Here are suggested activities for assessment:

Give me a . . . : Call out a number and have the children write that number (in numerals) inside the appropriate office. (Use blackline master 3.6 on page 96; an example is preprinted on the worksheet.)

From sticks to numbers: Show a set of craft sticks in a place-value house and have the children write the number it represents. A prepared worksheet is provided (blackline master 3.7 on page 97), or you could set up models using transparencies and craft sticks projected on an overhead projector.

Tens and ones: Call out a number as sets of tens and ones; for example, "two tens and five ones." Have the children write the corresponding number in numerals on a sheet of paper.

This number looks like . . . : Give each child a copy of blackline master 3.8 (page 98), which has blank place-value houses with numerals written underneath. The child draws sets of sticks to represent the numerals written below each house.

Chapter 4
Computation Using Place-Value Mats

Goals for This Chapter

1. To comprehend the meaning behind computation through representing it with actions
2. To become fluent in the process of computation
3. To learn to "make a ten" in addition
4. To learn to "take from ten" in subtraction

The purpose of this chapter is twofold. The first is for children to "see, hear, and do" the action of computing using place value, so that they comprehend the meaning behind computation. Second, we want them to become fluent in using place value, so that when they begin solving problems, they will not be distracted by having to concentrate on how to move through the steps of computation. The best way to accomplish both of these goals is to involve the students in action and story right from the start. The stories will provide a framework that explains why one does these steps and why they work, gives relevance to the practice, and provides a procedural memory prompt.

Every child will need place-value mats for ten and one (blackline masters 3.3a–b), 19 sticks, and a rubber band. As you tell the following story, the children will add and subtract sticks ("people") from their mats ("offices").

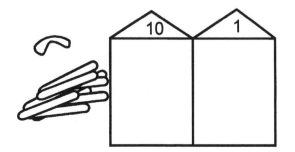

Story for Addition, or "Make a Ten"

You are the property manager for your offices. You drive up on the first morning, park your car, and unlock the front door of the ones side. (The tens side does not have a door!) You walk inside and check the offices. There are nine desks on the ones side and one conference table on the tens side that seats ten people. (More tables are stacked in the closet for later.) Everything is neat and clean. You are satisfied and proud.

Just then, the bell jingles on the door. You hurry over and see three people standing there. They shake your hand and tell you they want to rent office space. So you show them to three desks. (Have the children pick up three sticks and place them in the ones office.)

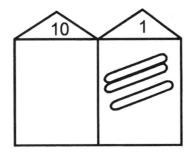

Just as you finish settling in your new people, the door opens and four more people walk in! (Have the children "walk" four more sticks into the ones office.) Stop at this point to discuss how many people are sitting in the ones office, presenting this as a simple sum (3 + 4 makes 7.)

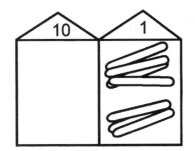

The bell jingles and four more people come in, smiling and shaking your hand. They want to rent space as well. (Have the children walk four more sticks into the ones side.) Wait a second to see if anyone says anything. If none of the children remark that there are too many people in the ones office, say, Oh, no! I hear a siren! We've got too many people in this office! I hear the planning commission coming! Hurry, let's get this sorted out. What shall we do?

If no one spontaneously says "make a ten," guide them to this solution. Prompt them to pick up ten sticks, rubber band them together, and quickly move them to the tens office. Emphasize the phrase "make a ten" because it will be useful throughout the teaching process.

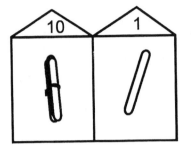

Again reassess the arrangement of the sticks. How many people are left on the ones side after the children made a ten? Guide students to recognize that there is ten and one more (10 + 1 = 11). Pause here to emphasize the "in and to the left" movement, which is a movement you want to ingrain in them. First they check the ones side, then they move to the left and check the tens side. When they say the number, however, they will name the tens first, then the ones. The movement is like the shape of a backwards numeral 7. Illustrate by drawing on the board or on your overhead, as shown in the following picture.

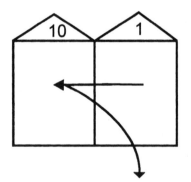

Now continue the story: "I hear the bell again! This time there are five people coming in the door! Where will you put them?" Guide the children to place the new people on the ones side. Then lead them to reassess the number in the offices now to see if they need to "make a ten" (11 + 5 = 16).

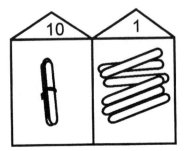

Continue the story, modeling simple addition through the actions of "come in, bundle, and move to the left" until you observe that the children no longer stop to ponder where to put their "people" and that they bundle tens together automatically. When they can do this confidently, it is time to move to the next section.

Activities for Math Centers

Place-value dot cards: Copy double-sided blackline master 4.1 (pages 99–100). Have children quiz each other about what number is represented by each dot card. (One child holds up a card, and the other child gives the answer.) For example, for 15, the child would say, "One 10 and five 1s." (Note that the ten shaded dots represent one bundle of ten.) If you photocopy the numbers on the back side of the dot cards, the partner holding up the card can see the answer. If you make duplicate sets of cards, students can use them to play memory or go fish. These cards can also be used for oral computation. After the child identifies the number represented, you could ask, "What would you have if I gave you three more? What would you have if I took four away?" and so forth.

Ones-place addition cards: The five double-sided pages of blackline master 4.2 (pages 101–10) contain simple sums that involve adding only in the ones place, without having to make a ten. Using their place-value mats and craft sticks, children can build the top number, then add sticks to represent the bottom number in order to determine the sum. They can also take turns drawing a card and solving the problem mentally. Because the answers are printed on the back, these cards are self-assessing if you copy both sides. If students need a prompt, encourage them to check their hands for the answer, rather than resorting to counting up. As discussed in book 1, children who become reliant on counting with their fingers have difficulty progressing beyond this strategy. Ignoring the tens column, students can use "my two hands" to determine the total in the ones column. (For more advanced problems, they can use "my two hands" one column at a time.) The beauty of this method is that children never need to master facts over ten in order to solve any problem.

Ones-place subtraction cards: The four double-sided pages labeled 4.3a–d (pages 111–18) are basic subtraction problems that do not require taking from the tens place. Laminate and cut apart the cards, then use them as described in the previous paragraph for addition cards.

Make-a-ten addition cards: The sums in double-sided blackline masters 4.4a–b (pages 119–22) require making a ten. It will be important to introduce these problems using the place-value mats. First the child would arrange sticks to represent the top number of the problem on the mat, then add the appropriate number of sticks for the bottom number of the problem. Remind the children, if necessary, that they need to "make a ten" and move it to the tens place mat. Then they can clear the mat, draw another card, and build the next problem.

Subtraction, or "Take from Ten"

Start with the children's place-value mats set up with 16 sticks (one 10 and six 1s) on them. (If you are continuing the lesson from the end of the story on page 22, there will already be 16 sticks on the place mats, or you could do a short addition story leading up to this sum.) As always, I use a story to introduce the new concept of taking from ten when there are not enough sticks in the ones office to subtract from there.

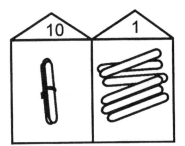

"Take from Ten" Story

You walk in the office door one morning and find that the air conditioning has broken and the office is hotter than hot! You choke and gasp and can hardly breathe! Just then five of the people start griping and complaining about how hot they are. You assure them you are going to fix the problem immediately, but they announce that they are leaving! They simply cannot work in that heat! You ask them to be patient, that you will work hard and fast to fix the problem, and soon the office will be nice and cool again. But they will not be consoled. They take their things and leave.

Processing: Ask the children where they would take the five people from. Guide them to look at the ones side first. You want to build a habit of checking the ones side first to determine whether there are enough "people" there from which to subtract the whole number.

Action: Having verified that there are enough people on the ones side from which to take five, have the class do so together.

Synthesis: Now have children examine what is left. In this case, there will be one 10 and one 1 like this: ▶

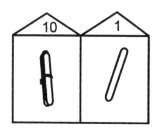

Story Continuation

On Monday morning when you come in the door, you smell a smell so horrible it almost makes you faint! You recover, though, and stagger around the office trying to find the source. Just then everyone walks in to start work. You see a paper lunch bag sitting on the floor where Ms. Green left it last Friday when she left in a huff over the broken air conditioning. You look inside and find that her tuna sandwich is rotten! Quickly you run the bag outside to the trash, but it's too late! The people who came in to start working are shouting, their faces are red, they are holding their noses and waving their hands. Four of them insist they will not stay one minute longer, even though you found the source of the smell and assure them you are taking care of the problem immediately! No! They grab their things and leave. (You check behind them to make sure no more lunches are left behind!)

Processing: Ask the children, "Where did these four people leave from? Are there enough people on the ones side for you to take four from? . . . No? . . . So where can we get four people? From the tens side? Yes! That's right. We can 'take from ten!'"

Action: Guide the children to unbundle their set of ten and remove four people. Watch to see what they do with the remaining six sticks. If they hesitate and appear to be thinking about what to do, let them puzzle for a bit. If they automatically start to put the six sticks back on the tens side, say, "I hear sirens!" Give the children every opportunity to figure out on their own that they cannot put the six sticks on the tens side anymore, and that they will need to be placed in the ones office.

Synthesis: When you have worked through this point, the place-value mats will look like the one below. Talk with the students about what happened, and assess the number they have left.

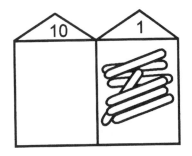

Continue with this type of storytelling until you see that the children automatically follow the correct procedure: they take from the ones side if there are enough there to do so. If not, they move to the tens. This is an important point to emphasize.

Math Center Games

Take-from-ten cards: Blackline masters 4.5a–c (pages 123–28) are similar to blackline master series 4.3, except that they require unbundling a ten. Have students set out the top number shown on the card on their place-value mats then subtract the bottom number. Doing so will require that they unbundle their ten, remove the correct number of sticks, and place the remaining sticks on the ones side.

Pattern discovery: To promote pattern discovery, you might place only the cards in which nine is subtracted in the math center. Observe whether the students notice that when they unbundle their ten and take nine away, they always have one stick left over. Thus the answer to any "subtract nine" problem is always going to be one more than the original number in the ones office. Do not actively attempt to teach this pattern. Just note whether any of the students catch on to this rule through playing with only the subtract nine cards. You could then proceed to providing only the subtract eight cards, then both subtract nine and subtract eight cards. The goal of this game is student discovery rather than active teaching.

Taking It Further

Working in small groups, lead the children to understand that the operations of "take from ten" and "make a ten" work exactly the same way for numbers larger than 20. Follow the steps in the "Story for Addition, or 'Make a Ten'" and "Subtraction, or 'Take from Ten'" sections, but this time, have two or more bundles in the tens office. Storytelling with more than one ten bundle will allow the students to recognize that the actions are identical for all computations using two digits, so once they have mastered this chapter, they will be able to do similar problems for numbers up to 99. I use the words "beginning," "action," and "ending" to help children identify the three components of a problem and determine the correct procedure to use.

Beginning = the initial number

Action = adding or subtracting

Ending = what is left after the action is completed

This language also makes a connection to word problems.

Beginning: Present a two-digit number.

Action: Add or subtract a one-digit number from the two-digit number. For example, you might start with three 10s and four 1s (see illustration). Present a story in which eight people want to leave (the action). First the children must check whether there are enough people in the ones office. No. So what do they do? Unbundle a ten and take eight from there. Then the two leftover sticks go on the ones side.

− 8

Ending: Assess what is left: "We used one 10 so that eight people could leave. That leaves us with two 10s in that office. There were already four people in the ones office, and now we have two more because there were two left over from the ten we unbundled."

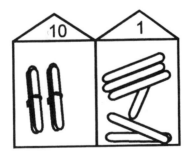

Point out that the action still makes the shape of a backwards numeral 7: (1) Check the ones side, (2) move to the tens and unbundle, and (3) put any leftover sticks in the ones office. Practice these types of problems until the children are fluent with procedures for addition and subtraction.

Subtracting Two-Digit Numbers

For a further challenge, set up the place-value mats with a number over 20 and lead students through subtracting a two-digit number, as described in the following example.

Beginning: Begin with two 10s and six 1s, as shown.

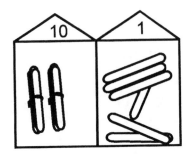

Action: Present an action that does not require unbundling a ten; for example, ask students to subtract 13, or one 10 and three 1s. Guide them to notice that they are doing exactly what you said: taking one 10 from the tens office and three 1s from the ones office.

Ending: Analyze the pattern of sticks that remains after the action is completed (see illustration):

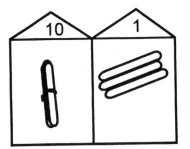

The value of proceeding all the way up to double-digit addition and subtraction is that students will not fear that computation will become harder as the numbers get bigger. If they gain mastery over the process for numbers below 20, they will have mastered the process for larger numbers as well. They can do it! This fact is empowering for all students but is especially critical for global learners.

Math Center Games

Double-digit addition cards: Use blackline masters 4.6a–b (pages 129–30). The child draws a card (for example, + 12) and sets up that number on a place-value mat. Drawing a second card, the child adds that number to what is already on the mat. Many problems will require bundling a ten as the ones side becomes too full. To help children manage the sticks without confusion, direct them to add the ones place of the second number to the ones side first, then assess whether they need to make a ten, before adding the tens (mirroring the process of traditional addition). For example, to add 19 to 12, the child adds nine to two, determines that the ones side is overfull, bundles and moves ten, then adds ten to the 20 already on the tens side. Then, leaving this set of sticks in place, the children can draw another card and add that number of sticks to those already on the mat.

Double-digit subtraction cards: The cards on blackline masters 4.7a–b (pages 131–32) work similarly to the addition cards, except the child should start with a very large number (such as 99) set up on the place-value mat. The child draws a card to subtract and starts by examining the ones side. Are there enough people in that office to take away the number in the ones place on the card? If so, the child simply takes the correct number of ones from the ones office and tens from the tens office. If there are not enough sticks on the ones side, the child can pick up the number of tens that will be subtracted plus one more to unbundle. Any leftover sticks from the unbundled ten go on the ones side. Allow plenty of practice with the addition and subtraction games.

Moneybags: Duplicate the pockets on blackline master 4.8 (page 133) and provide toy one- and ten-dollar bills. Label a series of items with prices in dollars only. (You could use empty food cartons, small toys, or simply pictures cut from catalogs and laminated.) The ones pocket functions just like the ones office, holding no more than nine dollars, and the tens pocket parallels the tens office. If you cut a slit partway along each pocket, the money can actually be placed in each pocket. One child pretends to be the customer and the other a sales clerk. The customer chooses a product to buy and checks the ones pocket first to see if there is enough money there. If not, the customer will need to make change for a ten in order to pay, and then put the change in the ones pocket. Introduce this game in a small group under your supervision until the children catch on. Then you can place the materials in the math center for independent use by pairs or small groups of children.

Assessments

Assessment worksheets (blackline masters 4.9a–c) are provided on pages 134–36, and a progress report and whole-class record listing the target skills for chapters 3 and 4 are provided in Appendix B (pages 206–7). Instructions are provided on the worksheets: The child looks at the offices, adds or subtracts the number shown, and draws the result in the blank place-value card below. You will have gained a great deal of awareness about what each child knows from observing and working with small groups, but these materials will provide the final test of what children know. I would recommend testing more than once in order to gain an accurate reflection of what the children know. As always, I believe the primary purpose of assessment is to identify any areas that may require further teaching. Note that blackline master 4.9b involves adding and subtracting double-digit numbers. The students can solve these problems using the strategies they already know, but for children who are easily intimidated, you may wish to present only the single-digit problems.

Chapter 5

A Bird's-Eye View

Goals for This Chapter

1. To discover patterns in computation to 20

2. To gain a global understanding of computation to 20

3. To learn motions associated with subtraction and addition

4. To apply prior knowledge of computation to 10 to problems up to 20

This chapter presents the bird's-eye, or global, view of computation with numbers to 20 using a chart that organizes everything in a gorgeous whole! Seeing all the facts to 20 will satisfy those learners who need to know how much there is to learn and reveals patterns that will facilitate learning. Paired with the chart are motions that will aid recall: the motion for subtraction is a downward sweep, while the motion for addition is an upward sweep. The format of the chart connects this new information to students' previous learning of the number houses (book 1, chapter 7). This chapter, in fact, begins with the tens facts, providing a familiar point of reference. The children will see the new number facts as a continuation of what they already know.

Locate the chart entitled "Computation to 20: a global view" (blackline master 5.1 on page 137) and enlarge it for class use. You also will want to make copies for individual student use. If you laminate them, these pages can be used with dry-erase markers for years. The teaching procedure works through one section at a time, beginning with oral, small-group discussion and discovery, then moving to written practice. I recommend having the students sit as close to you and the chart as possible, to maximize focus and engagement.

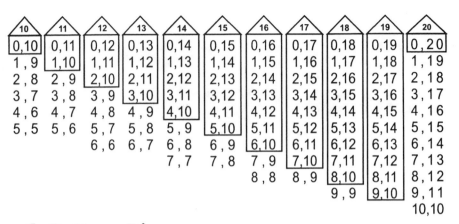

10	11	12	13	14	15	16	17	18	19	20
0,10	0,11	0,12	0,13	0,14	0,15	0,16	0,17	0,18	0,19	0,20
1,9	1,10	1,11	1,12	1,13	1,14	1,15	1,16	1,17	1,18	1,19
2,8	2,9	2,10	2,11	2,12	2,13	2,14	2,15	2,16	2,17	2,18
3,7	3,8	3,9	3,10	3,11	3,12	3,13	3,14	3,15	3,16	3,17
4,6	4,7	4,8	4,9	4,10	4,11	4,12	4,13	4,14	4,15	4,16
5,5	5,6	5,7	5,8	5,9	5,10	5,11	5,12	5,13	5,14	5,15
		6,6	6,7	6,8	6,9	6,10	6,11	6,12	6,13	6,14
				7,7	7,8	7,9	7,10	7,11	7,12	7,13
						8,8	8,9	8,10	8,11	8,12
									9,9	9,10	9,11
										10,10

Step 1: Pattern Discovery

1. Show the chart to the children and encourage them to talk about what they notice. Allow plenty of time for them to reflect. Record their responses.

2. Focus on the tens column, since the children are familiar with these problems. Point out that the ten is the attic number for this building. Explain to them that Stony Brook Village was growing so fast that the planning commission decided to build apartment buildings. Each building has an attic number, and each floor in the building has exactly that number of people. For example, in the tens building, each floor has ten people in it. Have the children verify that this is indeed true.

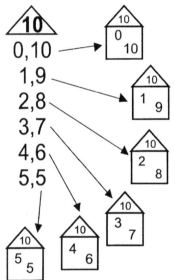

3. Using the chart, make an arc with one hand across the two numbers in one equation and up to the ten in the attic (see illustration). Associate this motion of an upward curve, which looks like a *C* or backwards *C*, with addition.

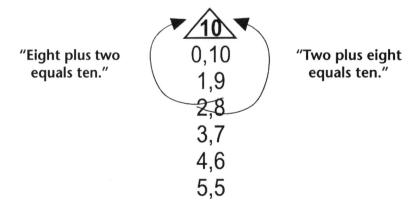

"Eight plus two equals ten."

"Two plus eight equals ten."

4. Have the children practice on their charts, reading an equation out loud while tracing the *C* or backwards *C* motion, moving upward from the lower numbers to the attic number.

5. For an additional connection between the motion and the action of addition, model saying, "Come here" while gesturing in an upward sweep with your arm. Describe addition as being like more people coming and joining the group.

come

6. Now demonstrate that the motion for subtraction is the opposite of that for addition: It is still a *C* or backwards *C*, but this time the motion is down and away. You could tie this to a movement of waving people away, which would make the group smaller.

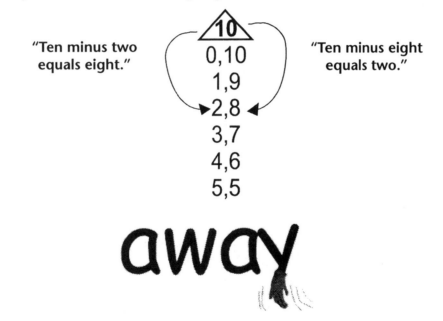

"Ten minus two equals eight."

$$\triangle 10 \triangle$$

0,10
1,9
2,8
3,7
4,6
5,5

"Ten minus eight equals two."

away

7. Have the children practice reading various equations while doing the addition or subtraction motions. I start with the familiar tens facts at this stage, so children focus on the movement cues, then move to other columns.

Step 2: Working with Ones

Draw attention to the fact that some of the floors in each building are enclosed in a box. Ask the children if they can guess why these floors are boxed. Give them time to brainstorm, and record their responses. Those floors in boxes are the problems that can be solved by adding or subtracting ones (that is, without making or taking from ten). Point out that the students already know how to do all those problems. Choose any problem inside a box and show them that they can simply add or subtract the ones without even touching the ten. (For example, 4 + 10 = 14 and 14 – 4 = 10.) The floors outside the boxes are the only problems that involve making a ten or taking from ten.

Practice

Oral practice: Give plenty of oral practice in solving problems inside the boxes. Look at a building, say number 13, and guide the children to recognize that each floor inside it is exactly like the threes houses, except that the 13 building has a ten sitting there. (That is, if the children ignore the numeral 1 in the tens place, the problems become 0 + 3, 1 + 2, 2 + 1, and 3 + 0, all of which they know.)

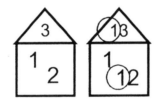

Written practice: Give the children worksheets that involve adding ones and taking from ones. (See blackline masters 5.2a–c and 5.3a–c, pages 138–43.) Work for mastery, confidence, and fluency with computation.

Assessments

Use the various pages of blackline masters 5.2 and 5.3 to assess the students' knowledge of the material in this chapter. Use more than one sheet in making this determination. In addition, a reproducible whole-class record sheet and progress report for use with chapters 5–7 are provided in Appendix B (pages 208–9).

Chapter 6
Make a Ten

Goals for This Chapter

1. To discover patterns in the global whole of math facts to 20

2. To determine how many equations there are for each number

3. To discover patterns that simplify problem solving

4. To gain fluency in solving problems that require "making a ten"

As I am writing today, I have goose bumps on my arms. This happens to me every time I immerse myself in the breathtaking patterns that exist within numbers. In this chapter, we will revisit the concept of "make a ten" using the global computation to 20 chart as a reference. (See page 137 for a copy.) We will be working only with addition in this chapter, and only with the problems outside the boxes on the computation chart.

Start out by having the children get out their charts. Remind them that they already know all the equations inside the boxes! This is very exciting! Guide them to the realization that they have already mastered far more problems than they have left to master.

Step 1: Pattern Discovery

Have the children examine the chart and discuss what they notice about the problems that lie outside the boxes. Allow plenty of time at this stage, as the children will be making discoveries and constructing meaning for themselves. Here are some patterns to explore:

1. Every column has an $n + 9$ equation right under its box (see illustration). Run a finger across the problems right under the boxes so the children will notice this pattern. Let the children connect all the $+ 9$ problems with a yellow colored pencil, then count how many of these problems there are to learn. They might be gratified to note that there are only eight! (**Note:** n is simply a convenient symbol to represent "any number." You would not, of course, use this symbol with the children.)

2. Point out that they will not need to study the houses labeled 10 and 20 because they have already learned the 10s house, and the 20s house is just like it except that there is an additional 10 in each row. The 19 building is not included either, because they already did that building as part of their adding ones practice (chapter 5, especially page 34).

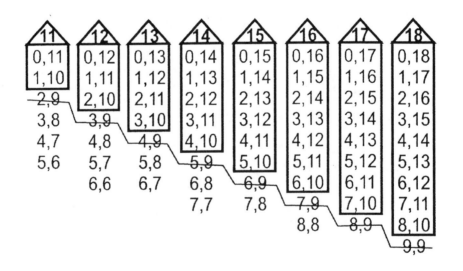

3. Now have the children locate the $n + 8$ problems, right under the $n + 9$ problems. Have them count how many there are. In a similar fashion, have them locate the $n + 7$ and $n + 6$ problems.

4. Next you might lead them to notice that the numbers added to each target number increase by one as you move right: **2** + 9, **3** + 9, **4** + 9, and so on. The children might want to circle this pattern with a red pencil.

5. Identify that the numbers on the left side of each building also increase by one as you go down the chart (mark with a green arrow pointing down), while on the right side of each building, the numbers increase going up (mark with a blue arrow going up).

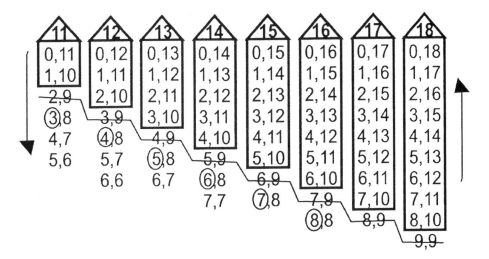

6. Now go back to the *n* + 9 problems. Guide the children into noting a relationship between this problem and the attic number: The ones place in the attic number is one number smaller than the number that is added to the nine. Have the children check all the buildings on the chart to verify that this pattern holds true.

Step 2: Make a Ten

Guide the students through oral practice with the "make a ten" problems in the houses, tying the equations to their previous practice with number houses and place-value mats.

Oral Practice

1. Starting with the 11 building, read the first equation under the box: "9 + 2 = 11," making a *C* motion with your hand, as described in chapter 5. Then do the same problem again, this time saying, "Nine 1s and two

1s is one 10 and one 1." Ask the children what happened to change the ones into a mix of tens and ones. Guide them to recognize that because there were more than nine 1s in the house, it was necessary to bundle and "make a ten."

2. Ask, "How many ones do we need to put with nine to make a ten?" If they hesitate, show them the 10s number house for 9 + 1 (see illustration). They can also look at their fingers, using the "my two hands" strategy to see how many they need to add.

3. You might also want to relate what they just did to their practice with place-value mats and bundling to make a ten, as well as the Stony Brook number houses.

4. Write an addition problem in the traditional vertical format with the larger number on top (see illustration). Direct the children to "pick up the top number" and take from the lower number what they need to make ten. As soon as they do that, they can write 1 in the tens place of the answer to represent one 10.

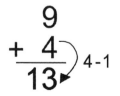

5. Next focus on the lower number and figure out how many are left after the children have taken from it to make ten. Write this number in the ones place below the line like this:

$$\begin{array}{r} 9 \\ +\ 4 \\ \hline 13 \end{array}\ 4\text{-}1$$

Written Practice

Give the children sheets of nines "make a ten" problems (blackline master 6.1, page 144). Have them practice until everyone can solve the problems fluently and confidently.

Finishing Up

Repeat the procedure described for the nines problems for eights problems (blackline master 6.2, the top half of page 145). Again, locate the problems, count how many there are, notice that the ones place in the attic number is always two digits smaller than the number being added to the eight. To connect this pattern with prior learning, draw the 2 + 8 number house. Guide students to recognize that they always will need to take 2 ones from the smaller number in order to make a ten out of the eight. Once the students seem confident with the eights problems, present a sheet of mixed eights and nines "make a ten" problems (blackline master 6.4, page 146).

Repeat the teaching process for the sevens equations (use blackline master 6.5, the top half of page 147), then present a mixed sheet of sevens and eights "make a ten" problems (blackline master 6.3, the bottom half of page 145) and sevens, eights, and nines "make a ten" problems (blackline master 6.7, page 148). Next teach the sixes "make a ten" equations (blackline master 6.6, bottom of page 147) and, when the children have mastered those, present a set of mixed problems adding numbers from six to nine (blackline masters 6.8a–b, pages 149–50). Continue practicing until the children can confidently solve all the problems outside the boxes on the computation chart.

Assessments

Use mixed-practice blackline masters 6.7, 6.8a, and 6.8b (pages 148–50) for formal assessment. Look for any consistent patterns of problems missed to identify individual children's needs for further practice. If necessary, go back to practice with concrete materials with children who are really stuck. Also remind the children that if they have difficulty remembering how many they need to add to a number to make ten, they can use the "my two hands" strategy to refresh their memories. A reproducible whole-class record sheet and progress report for use with chapters 5–7 are provided in Appendix B (pages 208–9).

Chapter 7
Take from Ten

Goals for This Chapter
1. To revisit number patterns within the global computation chart
2. To determine how many possible equations yield the same number
3. To discover patterns and connections to ease problem solving
4. To gain fluency in taking from ten

In this chapter, we focus on subtraction with the problems on the global computation chart that lie outside the boxes. When I think back to the time when my third graders were most likely to turn pale, it was always when they caught a glimpse of double-digit subtraction. There is something about this aspect of computation that strikes fear into the hearts of children. For this reason, we are going to carefully lay a good foundation for written double-digit subtraction. We do not want to lose any child at this point!

One thing we cannot do is succumb to the temptation simply to explain how to do subtraction. Expecting students to remember a series of steps they did not work through or discover for themselves will not work. Because some of the students will be unable to remember the steps, a verbal explanation does not save time in the long run. Instead we want to create an environment in which we can guide students to discover the action of the computation and to construct a procedure for themselves.

Step 1: Use Concrete Materials

Revisit the stories from chapter 4 in which the Stony Brook offices were plagued with disaster, causing some workers to leave (see pages 24–25). Provide place-value mats, craft sticks, and rubber bands for this review, and have the class physically work through the problems you choose. In your review, emphasize these points:

1. Subtraction involves people leaving.
2. Always check the ones side first to see if there are enough people there from which to take the ones who are leaving.
3. If not, you must take from ten by unbundling a ten and putting the remaining people in the ones office.

☆ ☆ ☆ TEACHING HINT ☆ ☆ ☆

On a large card, print

More (+) Means **Make** a Ten

Leave (–) Means **Take** from Ten

to remind the children that with addition more come in, so they make a ten, whereas in subtraction some leave, so they take from ten.

Step 2: Introduce Symbols

We will work through subtraction for one number at a time, so children have opportunities to discover the patterns that result from subtracting particular numbers. As with other steps in the *More Math, Please!* process, we will begin with pattern discovery, then use stories to provide a context for subtraction.

Pattern Discovery

1. Give each child a copy of the global computation chart you presented in chapter 5 (blackline master 5.1, page 137). Review how to use the chart for subtraction: The motion for subtraction is the opposite of that for addition: It is a *C* or backwards *C* starting at the attic number and moving down and over the two numbers that comprise the computation. You could tie this movement to waving people away, which would make the group smaller.

2. Refer to the global chart and locate the eight problems in the 11 to 18 columns that involve the number nine (the ones right below the boxes). Recall from chapter 5 that the problems below the boxes require using "make a ten" or "take from ten." Also recall that I do not focus on the 10, 19, and 20 columns because students have already learned those.

3. Write these problems on the board, leaving space between them. Make sure the children locate where these problems came from within the global chart:

$$
\begin{array}{cccccccc}
11 & 12 & 13 & 14 & 15 & 16 & 17 & 18 \\
-9 & -9 & -9 & -9 & -9 & -9 & -9 & -9 \\
\hline
\end{array}
$$

4. See if the children comment on the sequence of attic numbers. (Each number increases by one as they progress to the right.)

5. Ask them to make predictions about the answers. Do they think a pattern will appear in the answers as well as in the attic numbers? Record their thoughts, but do not actively teach the answers at this point.

Oral Computation

1. Starting with the first problem (11–9), ask the children, "What is happening in this story?" You want them to see the symbols but remember the action. For example:

    Beginning: The 11 is the beginning of the story: Say, "Once upon a time there were 11 people hard at work," or present a similar scenario.

    Action: Point to the "– 9" row of the problem and ask, "Something happened! What do you think happened in this second part of the story?" Let a volunteer invent a reason why nine people had to leave. (Maybe nine people broke out in a rash and had to go home!)

    Ending: The ending of the story is the number of people who stayed at work. With your help, the students will figure this out.

2. Ask, "From which office did the people leave?" guiding students to check the ones office first, then the tens office.

3. As soon as the class has identified that it will be necessary to "take from ten," cross out the numeral 1 in the tens place and the numeral 9, saying, "Those nine people left. How many were left over from the tens office?"

4. If the children reply correctly, ask where the one remaining person from the tens office will go now. As they answer "to the ones office," write "+ 1" by the right hand 1 of the 11.

5. Add the 1 + 1 in the ones office and write the answer below the line. This is the end of that story.

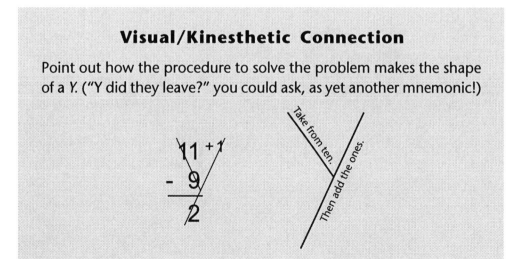

Visual/Kinesthetic Connection

Point out how the procedure to solve the problem makes the shape of a *Y*. ("Y did they leave?" you could ask, as yet another mnemonic!)

Move to the next problem (12 − 9) and repeat the process:

1. Ask, "What is the story?" (Twelve people were working, then nine left for some reason.)

2. Ask, "Can you take nine from the ones place? . . . No? So we take from ten and cross out the 1 in the tens place and the 9."

3. Ask how many are left after the people left the tens office. Write "+ 1" by the 2 in the ones place.

4. Complete the problem by adding the ones (that is, 2 + 1) and writing the answer.

Visual/Kinesthetic Connection for Self-Assessment

Point out that the top part of the *Y* shape used to solve the problem is like a *V*. This shape will help students to remember how to check their work. Starting at the top left, draw the downward stroke of a *V*, saying "ten minus nine." Then complete the upward stroke, saying "is one." The *V* can also be drawn the other direction, as shown on the right.

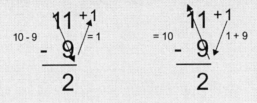

Step 3: Synthesize Learning

Complete the six other "subtract nine" problems in the same way. When all the problems have been solved on the board, ask whether the answers make a pattern:

- How do the answers compare to the attic numbers?
- Do you think that every time you subtract nine from a number, this pattern will appear? Why or why not?

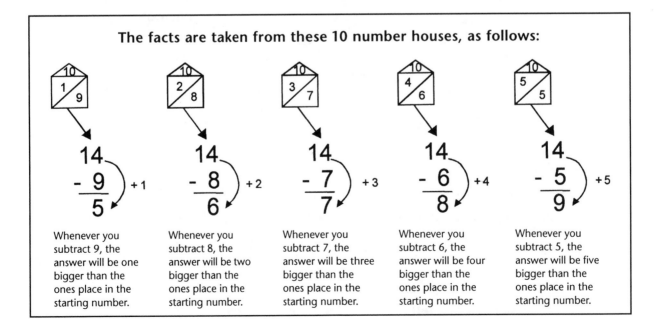

The facts are taken from these 10 number houses, as follows:

Whenever you subtract 9, the answer will be one bigger than the ones place in the starting number.

Whenever you subtract 8, the answer will be two bigger than the ones place in the starting number.

Whenever you subtract 7, the answer will be three bigger than the ones place in the starting number.

Whenever you subtract 6, the answer will be four bigger than the ones place in the starting number.

Whenever you subtract 5, the answer will be five bigger than the ones place in the starting number.

Step 4: Practice Written Computation

Blackline masters 7.1–7.8 (pages 151–58) provide written subtraction practice.

1. Start with blackline master 7.1, the nines "take from ten" problems. As students work, walk around and watch their progress, making notes about how each child is reacting to the work and solving the problems. Some children will move their pencils over each problem, mimicking the shapes you demonstrated, others will whisper the action to themselves, while others will simply look at the problem and quickly write the answer.

2. It is important at this stage to identify any child who is unable to do the work. If you realize that a child is struggling, work with him or her one-on-one:

    -   Provide concrete materials to manipulate and have the child talk through the action of each problem while you ask prompting questions if necessary.

    -   *Do not* repeat the story-explanation you gave to the class. If that explanation had made sense to the child, he or she would be able to solve the problems. It might be that the child has to construct a process that fits his or her own particular way of understanding.

    -   Encourage the child to talk about the problems until you identify the sticking point and can help him or her find a way to make sense of and recall the process.

3. Proceed through the remaining worksheets in this order:
    -   Blackline master 7.2, eights "take from ten" problems (page 152)
    -   Blackline master 7.3, eights and nines "take from ten" problems (page 153)
    -   Blackline master 7.4, sevens "take from ten" problems (page 154)
    -   Blackline master 7.5, sevens and eights "take from ten" problems (page 155)
    -   Blackline master 7.6, sevens–nines "take from ten" problems (page 156)
    -   Blackline master 7.7, sixes "take from ten" problems (page 157)
    -   Blackline master 7.8, twos–fives "take from ten" problems (page 158)

Assessments

When a student seems confident in completing blackline masters 7.1 to 7.8, use the four mixed subtraction problems worksheets (blackline masters 7.9a–d, pages 159–62) for assessment. Have the student complete more than one of these worksheets, so you can be sure of mastery. As always, your primary goal in assessment is not to assign a grade but to identify any lingering confusions or difficulties and provide remedial teaching as necessary until every child has achieved mastery. A reproducible whole-class record sheet and progress report for use with chapters 5–7 are provided in Appendix B (pages 208–9).

Chapter 8
Taking Stock

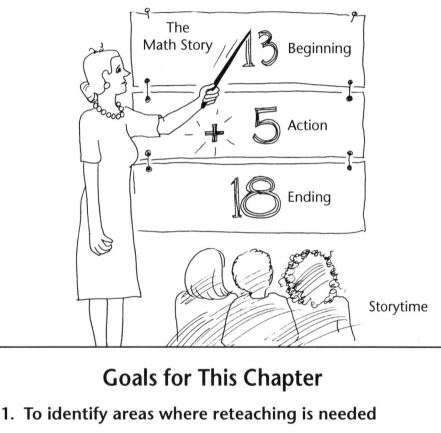

The Math Story

13 Beginning

+ 5 Action

18 Ending

Storytime

Goals for This Chapter

1. **To identify areas where reteaching is needed**
2. **To identify areas of mastery**
3. **To guide all students to fluency in solving varied problems**
4. **To review the three-part action of computation**

At this stage of the game, it will be important to take some time to determine how well your students have grasped the concepts you have presented. So before rushing on, let's allow all those busy brains to deepen their understanding and fluency. This chapter contains activities to build students' confidence and ease with computation, as well as assessments that should reveal exactly where they are in their understanding.

Step 1: Oral Discussion

I would recommend beginning math class every day with oral discussion of math problems, until the children are able to evaluate a problem quickly and determine what action is involved. The main goal of this activity is that each child learns to determine independently what action occurs in all types of addition and subtraction problems. Here is the procedure for oral discussion:

1. Choose a variety of addition and subtraction problems, both ones that require making or taking from ten and ones that add and take from ones.

2. Group the class around a chalkboard or white board, so everyone can see and participate easily.

3. Write the first problem on the board. I usually begin with an adding ones problem (that is, one that does not require making a ten), such as that shown in the following illustration. Ask, "What are the three parts of this story?" Ask leading questions as necessary to guide the students in talking through the problem, as shown in the following example:

13	**Part 1, Beginning:** We have 13, or one 10 and three 1s.
+ 5	**Part 2, Action:** Five more ones came in. We can add ones without making a ten.
18	**Part 3, Ending:** Now we have one 10 and we have eight 1s.

4. Write a "take from ones" problem (subtraction without taking from ten). To make the process as easy as possible, you may choose simply to rearrange the numbers from the first problem (see illustration). Again ask, "What are the three parts of the story?" The following is an example of the conclusions students would reach for this type of problem:

18	**Part 1, Beginning:** We have 18, or one 10 and eight 1s.
− 5	**Part 2, Action:** Five 1s leave. We can take from the ones.
13	**Part 3, Ending:** Now we have one 10 and we have three 1s.

5. Next present a "make a ten" problem and talk through the same steps of finding and describing the three story parts, as shown in the illustration:

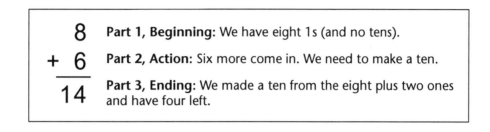

> **8**
>
> **+ 6**
> _____
> **14**
>
> **Part 1, Beginning:** We have eight 1s (and no tens).
>
> **Part 2, Action:** Six more come in. We need to make a ten.
>
> **Part 3, Ending:** We made a ten from the eight plus two ones and have four left.

6. Finally, give an example of a "take from ten" problem, as shown in the following illustration:

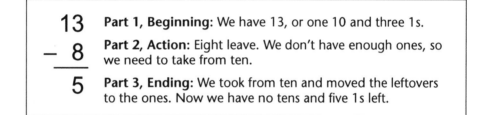

> **13**
>
> **− 8**
> _____
> **5**
>
> **Part 1, Beginning:** We have 13, or one 10 and three 1s.
>
> **Part 2, Action:** Eight leave. We don't have enough ones, so we need to take from ten.
>
> **Part 3, Ending:** We took from ten and moved the leftovers to the ones. Now we have no tens and five 1s left.

7. Now that you have presented a representative problem of each type, continue by presenting a random mix of problems.

Step 2: Oral Assessment

Make up flash cards representing all four types of story actions. Have one child at a time come to your desk. Take five minutes with the child, asking him or her to describe the story for each problem. Make notes about your assessment of the child's understanding and competency. A whole-class record and individual progress report applicable to the four types of problems can be found in Appendix B (pages 210–11). Identify children who need more practice in a specific area, and meet with these children in a small group for more oral practice.

Step 3: Written Practice

The purpose of presenting written problems is to determine whether all the students can identify the right procedure to use for each problem when they have a sheet of mixed problems. Lead into the worksheets with a brief oral discussion of the different problem types, as described previously. Then give the children the following worksheets in the order specified:

- Mixed addition and subtraction in ones place (blackline masters 8.1a–f, pages 163–68)

- Mixed addition and subtraction of nines (blackline masters 8.2a–b, pages 169–70)

- Mixed addition and subtraction of eights (blackline masters 8.3a–b, pages 171–72)

- Mixed addition and subtraction of sevens (blackline masters 8.4a–b, pages 173–74)

- Mixed addition and subtraction of sixes (blackline masters 8.5a–b, pages 175–76)

- Mixed addition and subtraction, sixes–nines (blackline masters 8.6a–c, pages 177–79)

- Mixed addition and subtraction, twos–fives (blackline masters 8.7a–b, pages 180–81)

- Mixed addition practice (blackline masters 8.8a–b, pages 182–83; these worksheets contain a mix of "make a ten" and "add ones" problems)

- Mixed subtraction practice (blackline masters 8.9a–b, pages 184–85; these worksheets contain a mix of "take from ten" and "take from ones" problems)

- Mixed addition and subtraction practice (blackline masters 8.10a–b, pages 186–87; these worksheets contain a mix of all four actions: add ones, make a ten, take from ones, and take from tens.

Step 4: Written Assessment

Once the students have completed this series of worksheets, you should be able to identify each child's level of understanding from the patterns of errors. Use these worksheets to identify each child's need for further teaching. Group children according to the concepts they need to review and provide small-group practice until they can solve the problems automatically without hesitating to decide what to do. When the children demonstrate mastery, proceed to multi-digit computation in chapter 9. For the most efficient progress, it is critical not to move on to chapter 9 until the children are confident in solving all the problems presented thus far.

Chapter 9
To the Top!

Goals for This Chapter

1. **To provide extension activities as appropriate**
2. **To show the similarity in procedure between computing with small and large numbers**

I will never forget arriving at this moment with my kindergarten group last year, seeing those little faces with their chubby cheeks, their eyes full of wonder over what they could do with really *big* numbers. Children find something magical about numbers that are enormous. And when they find out that they can work with and solve problems using these numerical giants, their awe and pride know no bounds. In this chapter we will apply the same procedure students have already mastered to larger numbers.

Note: It is essential that all the children be comfortable with the work to this point before you introduce the activities in this chapter.

Adding and Subtracting Ones

I begin by drawing the class together in a close group, then writing a double-digit addition problem such as this one on my board:

$$\begin{array}{r} 23 \\ +42 \\ \hline \end{array}$$

1. I ask the class whether they can solve this problem. When they say, "No," I reply, "I believe you can!" I let them look at the problem for a few seconds, just waiting to see what their comments will be.

2. Then, drawing a vertical line between the offices, I ask, "How many ones are there?"

3. When they answer this question (five), I ask, "How many tens are there?"

4. As the children answer, I write the numbers on the board.

$$\begin{array}{r} 2\,|\,3 \\ +4\,|\,2 \\ \hline 6\,|\,5 \end{array}$$

5. Next I choose another, similar problem that involves adding or subtracting ones and tens, but does not involve *making or taking from ten*.

6. I continue this exploration with the children until they realize that all they are doing is adding or subtracting numbers less than ten.

Oral Practice

1. Write multi-digit problems on the board and have the children discuss the answer in a group. Begin with a set of three-digit numbers that they can easily add column-by-column without making or taking from ten, such as the following:

$$\begin{array}{r} 241 \\ +314 \\ \hline 555 \end{array}$$

2. Then write a problem with four-digit numbers and repeat. Continue this way as long as the children are engaged and are enjoying this activity.

Written Practice

Copy and hand out any of the basic multi-digit addition and subtraction worksheets (blackline masters 9.1a–e, pages 188–92). I have included a series of these sheets that involve progressively larger numbers, but do not require making or taking from ten. Don't be surprised if you have some students who simply must find out how large the problem can get and still have this method work. Two of my students grappled with this process for a whole morning and were not satisfied until they had me turn the paper sideways and write problems that stretched the entire width of the page. When they found that this method worked even for problems that were about ten inches wide, they finally gave up. I like to imagine that they assumed at this point that there were no larger numbers, since we had used up the whole width of the paper!

Double-Digit Make a Ten

1. Show the children a problem that requires making a ten, such as the following. Discuss the "story" of this problem, using the procedure given in chapter 8.

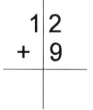

2. Once the class has determined that the action requires them to make a ten, ask them how many tens they will have once they make the new ten (two). Write the answer as they respond.

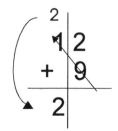

3. Next, ask them how many are left on the ones side, now that they had to take some to make a ten.

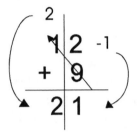

4. Guide them to reason that they took one from the two to make the ten, and now they have only one left. As the discussion proceeds, write "– 1" (to symbolize the one taken from the two), then the answer at the bottom.

5. Recap the action: "We already had a ten on the tens side, then we made another ten out of the nine plus one more. That gave us two tens, and then we had only one left over in the ones office. We wrote that one on the ones side of the answer."

6. Continue to present similar problems until the children demonstrate that they understand what to do. I would suggest using problems such as these:

16	13	25	28	36	43
+ 9	+18	+15	+25	+28	+38

7. Talk through each problem in turn, modeling the steps on the board, as illustrated:

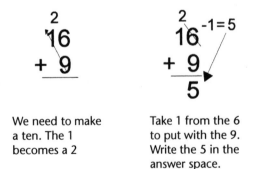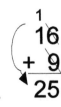

We need to make a ten. The 1 becomes a 2

Take 1 from the 6 to put with the 9. Write the 5 in the answer space.

Write the 2 tens in the answer space.

8. Continue in this fashion until the children are comfortable with the procedure and clearly understand what they are doing. If they understand the procedure, they will fall into problem-solving strategies that work well for them.

Work with Partners

Have the children work in pairs, taking turns solving double-digit problems. The child who is solving the problem talks through the process aloud. Meanwhile, the partner listens and monitors the first child's problem solving.

Written Practice

Locate the blackline masters labeled "Double-digit make a ten" (blackline masters 9.2 a–c, pages 193–95). Give the children half-sheets at first, explaining that when they finish that sheet, they are free to ask for more. Over time, the children will work more and more quickly, starting to do steps in their heads rather than on paper, until finally they can solve these problems entirely in their heads. This fluency results not from a lot of teaching, but from a lot of practice.

Single-Digit Take from Ten

Begin by talking through several problems as a class. Then, once the children are comfortable with the procedure, progress to written work.

Oral Introduction

1. Group the children around a white board or chalkboard. On the board, write a "take from ten" problem (see example).

2. Talk through the problem-solving process by way of review:

$$
\begin{array}{r}
13 \\
-\ 8 \\
\hline
\end{array}
$$

- In this problem, the ten will disappear right away because we will need to take the eight from it.

- The two ones that are left will go into the ones office.

- Remind children of the Y-shaped action employed to solve this problem.

3. Leaving this solved problem on the board, write another one for which the answer is exactly ten different from the previous problem (as illustrated):

$$
\begin{array}{r}
23 \\
-\ 8 \\
\hline
\end{array}
$$

4. Have the students establish that taking from ten is necessary. Ask, "If I take a ten so that I can subtract the eight, how many tens will be left?" (one) Write that in the answer space.

5. Next, place the leftover ones on the ones side:

6. Now evaluate how many ones there are and write the answer. Your problem will look like this:

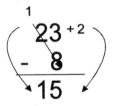

7. Discuss motions that the students might use as mnemonics for solving this type of problem. If they determine that they will need to take a ten, you could slash through both the tens place and the number being subtracted. The next action could become a backwards *C* as you write the new tens-place number at the top, write the + 2 on the ones side, and then go to the bottom to write the answer.

8. At this point, write the problem 33–8 on the board and let the children predict what the answer will be. Solve this problem and compare the three answers. See if the children detect a pattern and can explain why this pattern is occurring. (The ones place of the answer remains constant because the ones in the problem do as well. The answer in the tens place becomes one larger each time, just as the tens place of the number being subtracted from does.)

Synthesis

1. Write about five problems side-by-side on the board. Make the top number the same in each problem, but have the number being subtracted change by one from problem to problem (for example, – 9, – 8, – 7, – 6, and – 5). Solve these problems together and discuss the answers. Here are some tips students can use to self-check their answers:

    • When you take from ten, the answer in the tens place will always be one smaller than the starting number.

    • When you take from ten, the ones side will always become larger because you put your leftovers there.

2. Construct the following chart, with the students helping to determine these facts:

> ■ If you take away nine, the ones side will increase by one (10 – 9 = 1 and 9 + 1 = 10).
>
> ■ If you take away eight, the ones side will increase by two (10 – 8 = 2 and 8 + 2 = 10).
>
> ■ If you take away seven, the ones side will increase by three (10 – 7 = 3 and 7 + 3 = 10).
>
> ■ If you take away six, the ones side will increase by four (10 – 6 = 4 and 6 + 4 = 10).
>
> Continue for all the numbers to one.

3. Now write the following problem on the board:

$$\begin{array}{r} 33 \\ -\ 8 \\ \hline \end{array}$$

4. Have the children predict the answer, giving them plenty of time to think before you step in. If they are able to solve the problem mentally, proceed to the problem given in step 5. If they cannot solve mentally, ask questions to guide them through the steps:

   - "What action is involved?" (take from ten)
   - "How many tens are left?" (two) Write 2 by the tens.
   - "How many ones are left ?" (two) Write 2 next to the ones side.
   - "How many ones are there all together?" (five) Write the answer.

5. Next present the problem 43 – 8. Most likely the children will have the pattern down by now and will be able to state the answer. If they have difficulty, talk them through the steps as before. If any children hesitate over the answer, present the next problem in the series (53 – 8). Once the children are able to solve problems in this pattern confidently, write a mixture of take-from-ten problems, such as the following. Talk through the answers as a class.

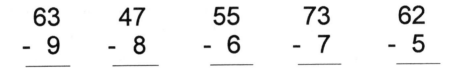

$$
\begin{array}{ccccc}
63 & 47 & 55 & 73 & 62 \\
-\ 9 & -\ 8 & -\ 6 & -\ 7 & -\ 5 \\
\hline
\end{array}
$$

Written Practice

Locate blackline master 9.3, labeled "Single-digit take from ten" (page 196). This page can be cut in half and presented one half at a time. Stay at this level for however long it takes for the children to become fluent with this type of problem. To be sure they have mastered the work to this point, give them a sheet of mixed problems (blackline master 9.4 on page 197).

Double-Digit Take from Ten

These problems are much more complex, so introduce them slowly with oral practice at the beginning of each math lesson for several days. In actuality, the only added step is that tens are being subtracted in two places: first you take a ten to make enough ones, then you take however many tens are needed for the digit in the tens place. You may wish to stress this idea after you have worked a problem or two on the board.

Oral Introduction

1. Begin with the following problem:

$$
\begin{array}{r}
26 \\
-19 \\
\hline
\end{array}
$$

2. Ask the children to comment on what they see in the problem and how they might go about solving it. See whether any of the students recognize that they will need to take one of the tens from which to subtract the nine, then use the other ten for subtracting the ten on the tens side. Use arrows to illustrate this process.

3. Once the tens are gone, all that remains to be done is to put the leftover one (after taking nine from the ten) with the six and write the answer:

4. Evaluate the following problems, talking through the steps together in the same way:

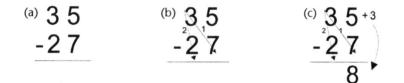

   a. Take from ten because there aren't enough ones.

   b. How many tens are we taking away? (Two full and one partial.) We write a small 2 for the two 10s the problem says to take away, and 1 for the one 10 we unbundle. We add 2 + 1 to get the number of tens we subtract. Are there any tens left? If so, write that number in the answer spot.

   c. Leftover ones go in the ones side. Now add up the ones and write the answer on that side.

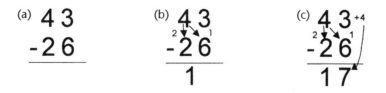

   a. Take from ten because there aren't enough ones.

   b. How many tens are we taking away? (Two full and one partial.) We write a small 2 for the two 10s the problem says to take away, and 1 for the one 10 we unbundle. We add 2 + 1 to get the number of tens we subtract. Are there any tens left? If so, write that number in the answer spot.

   c. Leftover ones go in the ones side. Now add up the ones and write the answer on that side.

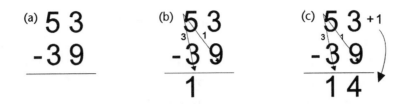

a. Take from ten because there aren't enough ones.

b. How many tens are we taking away? (Three full and one partial.) We write a small 3 for the three 10s the problem says to take away, and 1 for the one 10 we unbundle. We add 3 + 1 to get the number of 10s we subtract. Are there any tens left? If so, write that number in the answer spot.

c. Leftover ones go in the ones side. Now add up the ones and write the answer on that side.

5. Some children prefer to place the leftover ones on the ones side before dealing with the tens side, which is fine. As teachers, our job is to be sure the children understand the problem-solving procedure, because once they do, they will develop their own personal steps for solving the problems. We want each child to discover what works for him or her. Allow the students to practice repeatedly without pressure so they develop their own system.

Practice with Partners

Copy and cut apart blackline master 9.5, entitled "Double-digit take from ten" (page 198). Present a half-worksheet at a time, and have children work in pairs to solve these problems. One child talks through the process of solving a problem while the other child observes and offers feedback. Then the partners can switch roles.

Written Practice

Let each child independently complete the same half-sheets (blackline master 9.5, page 198). As always, analyze the corrected papers to determine where each child needs more practice. Continue providing similar problems until the child appears to have mastered this problem type. Then provide at least two half-sheets of mixed problems for formal assessment. (Use blackline master 9.6, page 199.)

At the Top! Multi-Digit Computing

In the final section, we will present three-digit addition and subtraction problems. As before, begin by discussing the problems as a group, then move to small-group practice and written practice before finishing with formal assessment.

Oral Practice for Addition

1. Begin by presenting a problem such as this: ▶

$$\begin{array}{r} 2\,3\,7 \\ +3\,8\,9 \\ \hline \end{array}$$

2. Evaluate the problem together. Don't write anything yet, just discuss what will happen in solving the problem:

   - Establish that the only difference between three-digit computation and the problems the students already know how to solve is that there is one more column of numbers. The process is still identical.

   - Look for places where making a ten will be necessary; namely, in the ones column and the tens column.

   - Next, note that the students will have to take some ones from the smaller number to make a ten. In the ones column, the seven will become 7 – 1, and in the tens column, the three will become 3 – 2. But then, remember that in making a ten, one more ten will show up in that column.

3. Now work through the computation step by step:

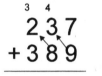

We will have to make a ten and make a 100 in the first two columns. Let's go ahead and bundle, changing the numbers like this: adding a ten to the middle digit changes the 3 to a 4, and adding one 100 to the 100s office changes the 2 to a 3.

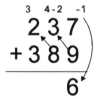

Now let's write down what we took from the smaller number in each column to make our ten and 100. On the ones side, we had to take one from the 7 to go with the 9. And in the tens office (the middle numbers), we had to take 2 from the 4 to go with the 8.

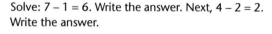

Solve: 7 – 1 = 6. Write the answer. Next, 4 – 2 = 2. Write the answer.

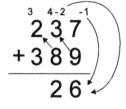

Now all we have to do is to add the last column. 3 + 3 = 6, which we write in the answer space.

If the children prefer to bundle first, then take from the smaller numbers, the steps are very similar.

1. Bundle the columns that need bundling, changing the top numbers to reflect this action.

2. Write the minus numbers by the top numbers ($4-2$ in the tens column; $7-1$ in the ones column).

3. Solve each column, starting on the right. Write the answers in the answer field.

4. You're all done! Notice that the action forms a series of backslash lines, then arcs to the sides of the problem.

Work through problems aloud as a group until the children quickly see what they need to do.

Practice and Assessment

1. Have pairs of children work through problems together, as described in previous sections of this chapter.

2. Next have children solve the same or similar problems independently. Review their work to identify any misunderstandings requiring reteaching.

3. Finally, use the two half-worksheets labeled "Multi-digit make a ten" (blackline master 9.7, page 200) for formal assessment.

Oral Practice for Subtraction

1. As always, begin with oral group discussion of a problem such as the following:

$$\begin{array}{r} 743 \\ -156 \\ \hline \end{array}$$

2. Before writing anything, discuss the problem and what actions will be necessary in solving it: Starting on the right, ask if they can take the six from the three. No, so they will have to take numbers from somewhere. Next, look at the tens office. Ask whether they can take the five from the four. No! So they will need to go next door again and unbundle a 100!

3. Now that the children see what's in store, talk through solving the problem step by step, as shown in the example on the following page.

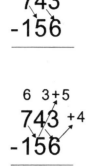

Evaluate: We cannot take 6 from 3 nor 5 from 4. But we can take 1 from 7. Draw lines through the numbers you are taking away from, like this, and write the new number above the old one.

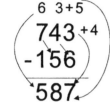

Next, put the leftovers by each top number. When you take 6 from 10, there will be 4 left over, so write + 4 by the 3. Notice the V shape you make when figuring out the leftover units.

Now let's solve! 3 + 4 is 7, and 3 + 5 is 8, so we can write those in the answer spaces. Finally, we solve for 6 – 1 in the hundreds office and write that answer as well.

Some children may prefer to work one *V* at a time—slashing through the four tens and six ones, then writing the four leftover ones—before moving to the hundreds office. They would then slash through the seven and the five and write the leftover units (+ 5) in the tens place.

As before, have the children practice with a partner first, then solve written problems independently. When your informal evaluation indicates that each child has mastered these problems, present the two halves of blackline master 9.8 (labeled "Multi-digit take from ten," page 201) for formal assessment. See Appendix B (pages 210–11) for a whole-class record and progress report.

Conclusion

Enjoy yourself. Encourage your students to decide now and then what math work they would like to do that day. I suspect you will find that they ask for specific areas in which they need more fluency. I would suggest keeping cubbies in the room with prepared sheets for each type of problem. On "free math day," students can simply choose whichever sheets they want to review. Allowing students to choose the math work they do is very empowering for them. They will delight in making decisions for themselves within the parameters you set for them.

Appendix A
Reproducible Blackline Masters

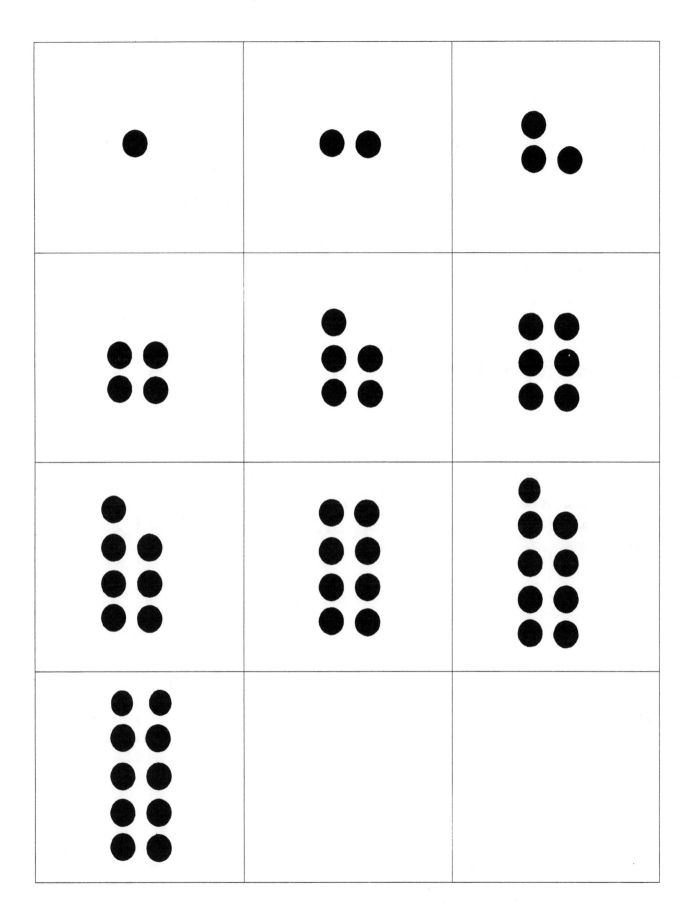

2.1. Dot cards

1	2	3	4	5
6	7	8	9	10
11	12	13	14	15
16	17	18	19	20
21	22	23	24	25
26	27	28	29	30
31	32	33	34	35
36	37	38	39	40
41	42	43	44	45
46	47	48	49	50
51	52	53	54	55
56	57	58	59	60
61	62	63	64	65
66	67	68	69	70
71	72	73	74	75

1	2	3	4	5
6	7	8	9	10
11	12	13	14	15
16	17	18	19	20
21	22	23	24	25
26	27	28	29	30
31	32	33	34	35
36	37	38	39	40
41	42	43	44	45
46	47	48	49	50
51	52	53	54	55
56	57	58	59	60
61	62	63	64	65
66	67	68	69	70
71	72	73	74	75

2.2. Fives-frame number chart

More Math, Please! Numbers over 10, © 2002 Zephyr Press, Tucson, AZ • 800-232-2187 • www.zephyrpress.com

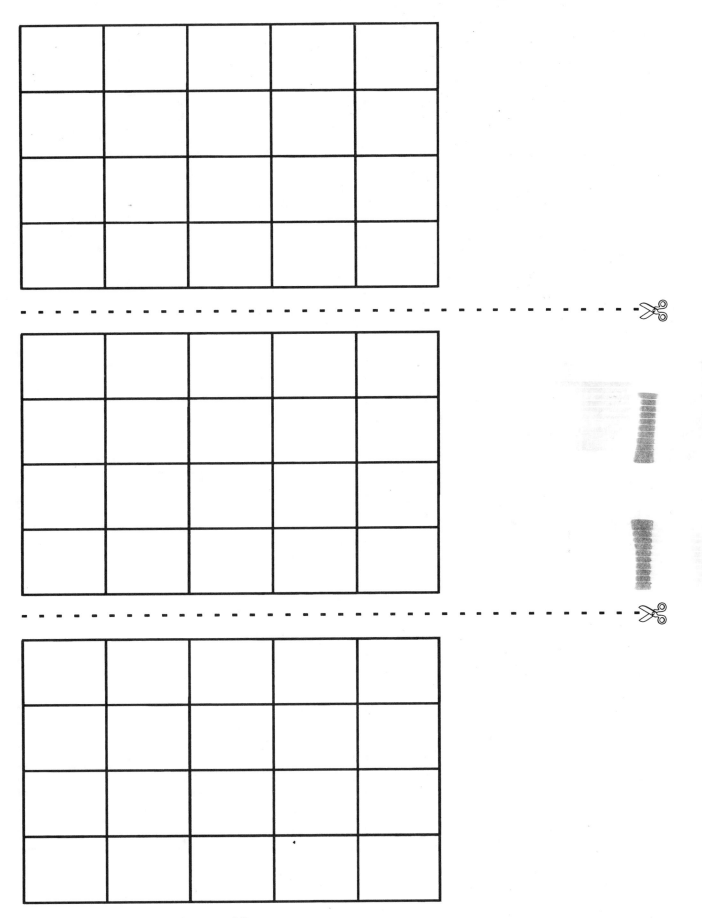

2.3. Blank fives-frame chart to 20

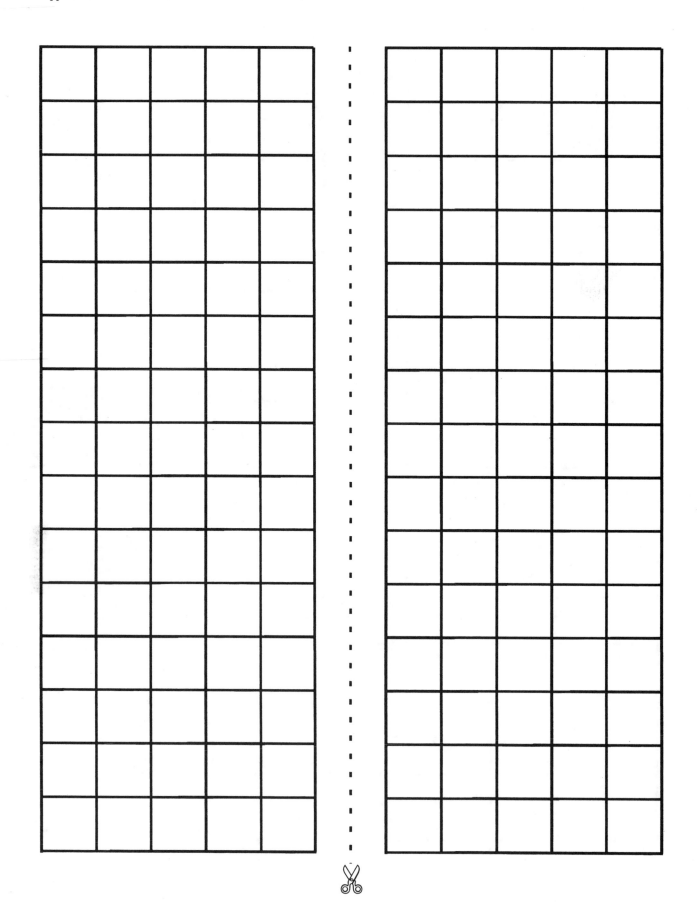

2.4. Blank fives-frame chart

 More Math, Please! Numbers over 10, © 2002 Zephyr Press, Tucson, AZ • 800-232-2187 • www.zephyrpress.com

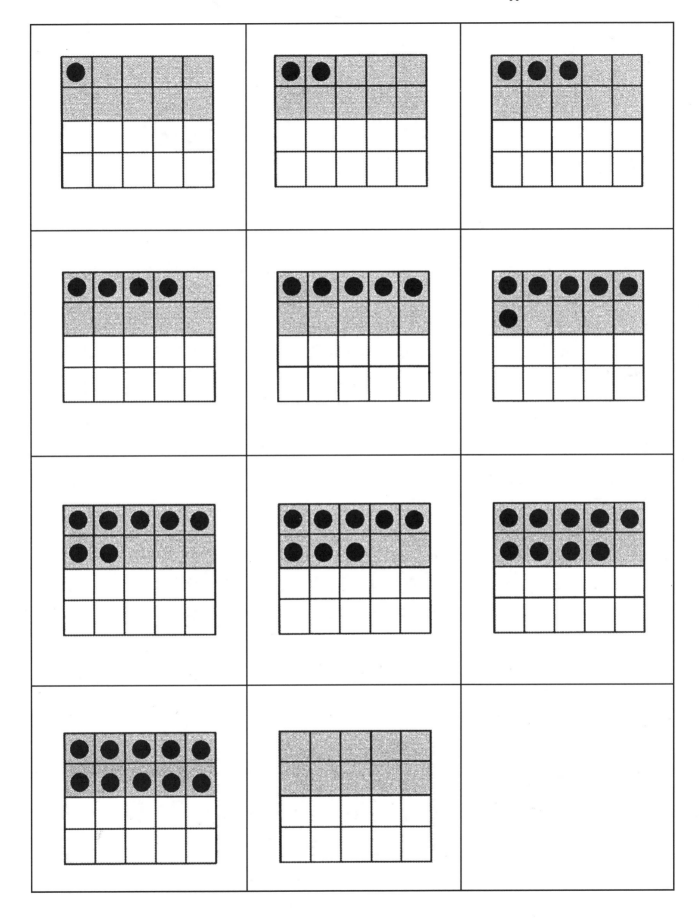

2.5a. Fives-frame dot cards, page 1

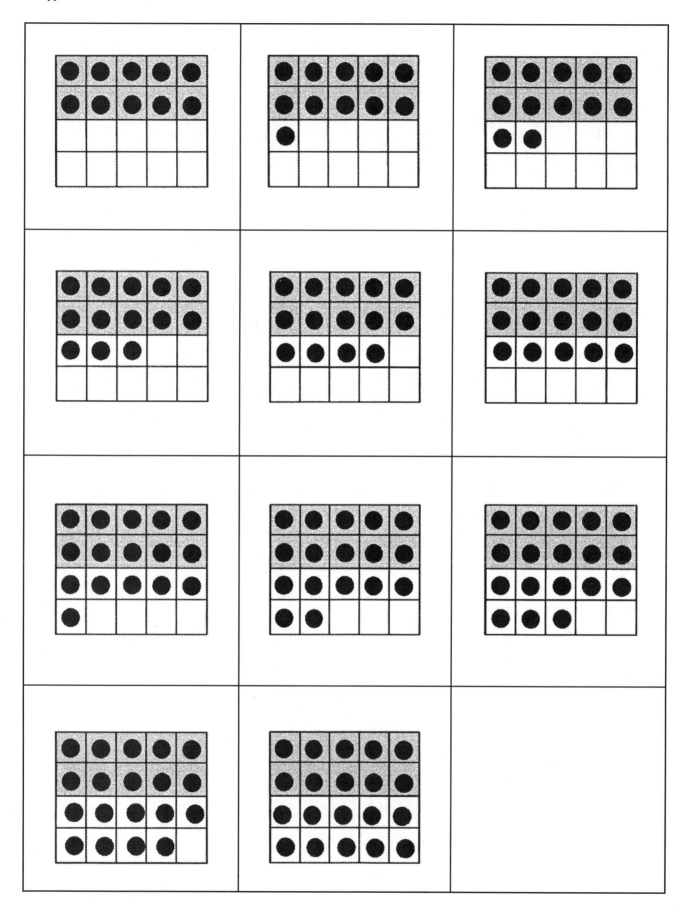

2.5b. Fives-frame dot cards, page 2

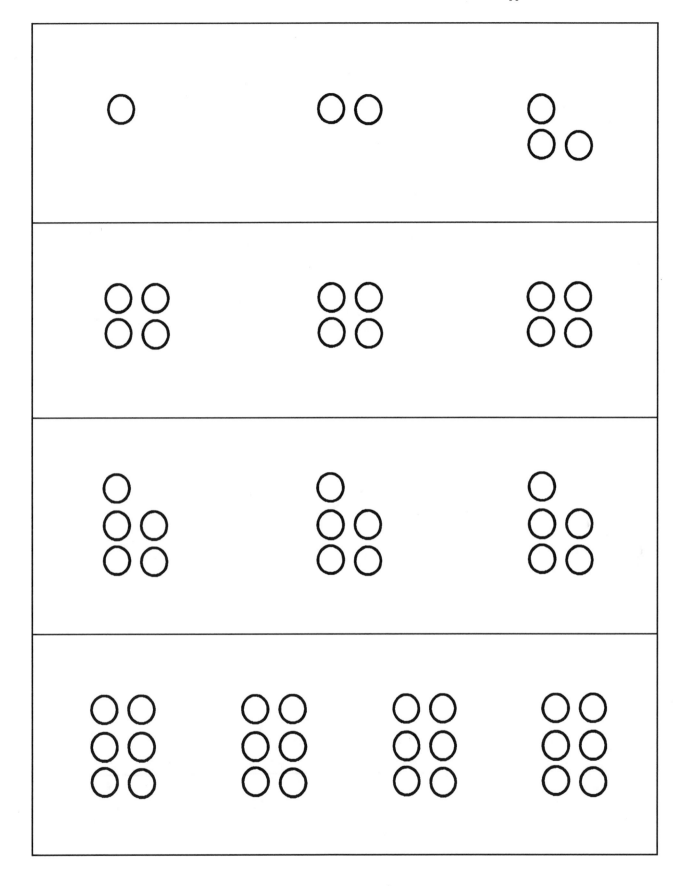

2.6a. Hollow dot cards, page 1

2.6b. Hollow dot cards, page 2

 More Math, Please! Numbers over 10, © 2002 Zephyr Press, Tucson, AZ • 800-232-2187 • www.zephyrpress.com

2.7a. Threes

Figure out which families can live in each house.

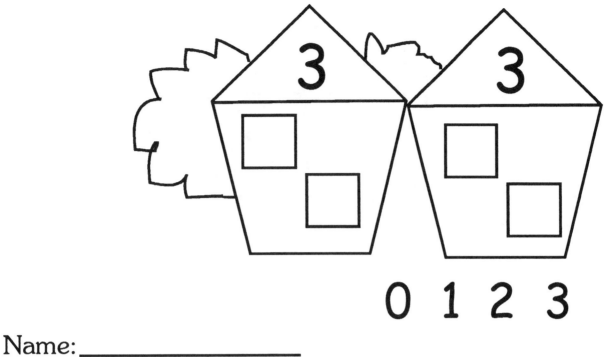

0 1 2 3

Name:_____

. . . .

2.7b. Fours

Figure out which families can live in each house.

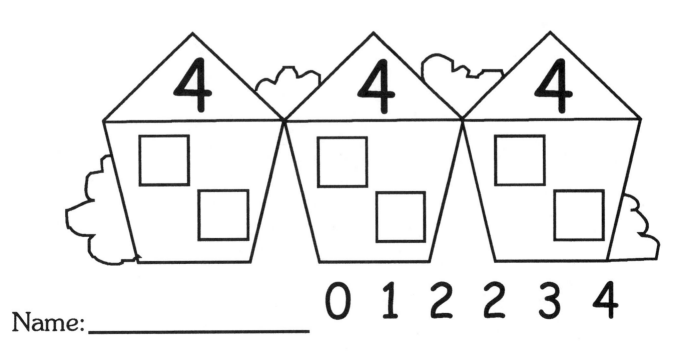

0 1 2 2 3 4

Name:_____

Name: _____

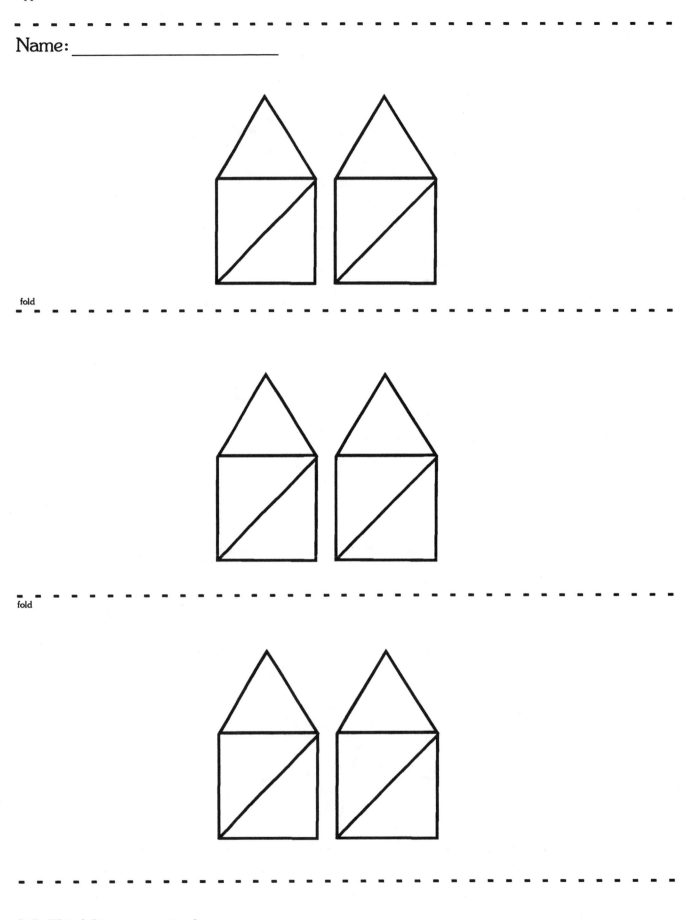

fold

fold

2.8. Third Street practice houses

Name:_____

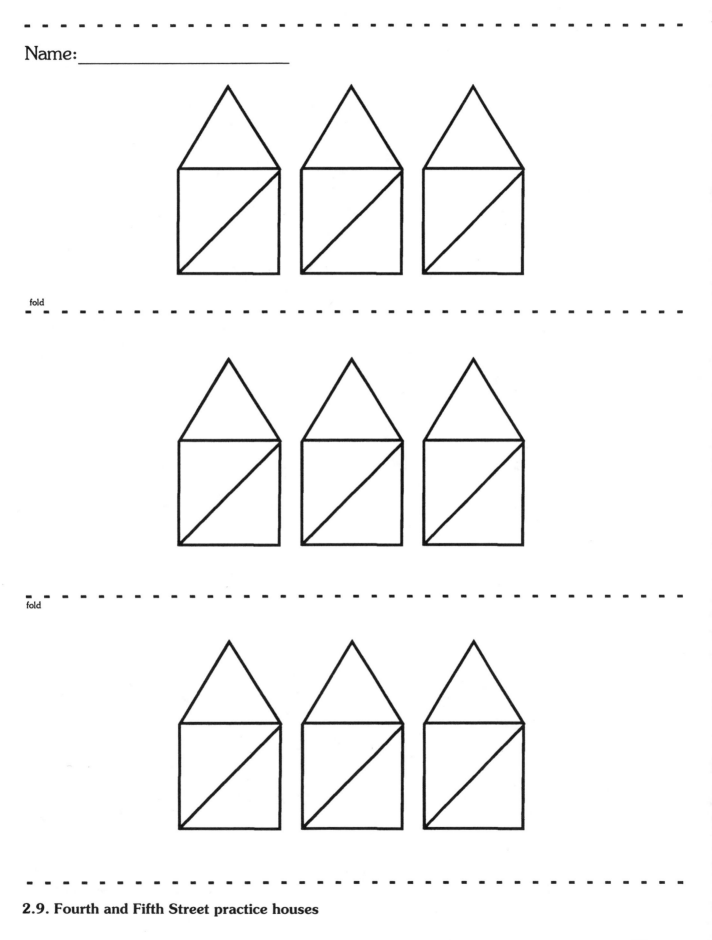

fold

fold

2.9. Fourth and Fifth Street practice houses

2.10. Addition and subtraction practice, threes and fours

Name:_____

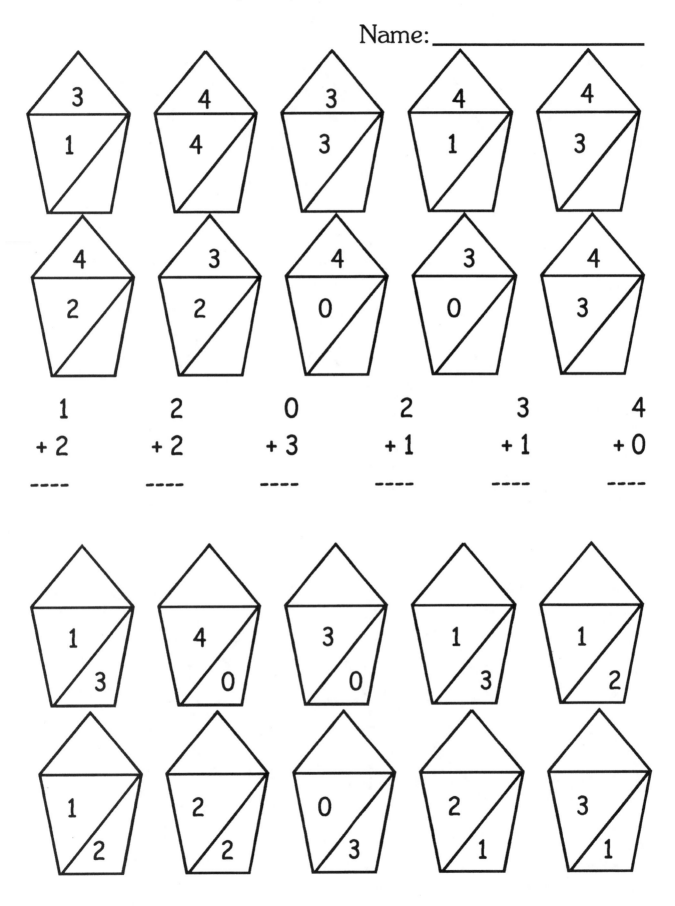

2.11a. Fives

Figure out which families can live in each house.

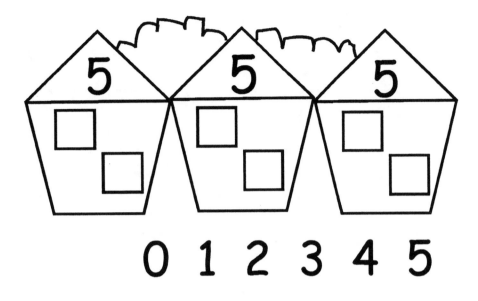

Name:_____

. . . .

2.11b. Sixes

Figure out which families can live in each house.

Name:_____

Name: _____

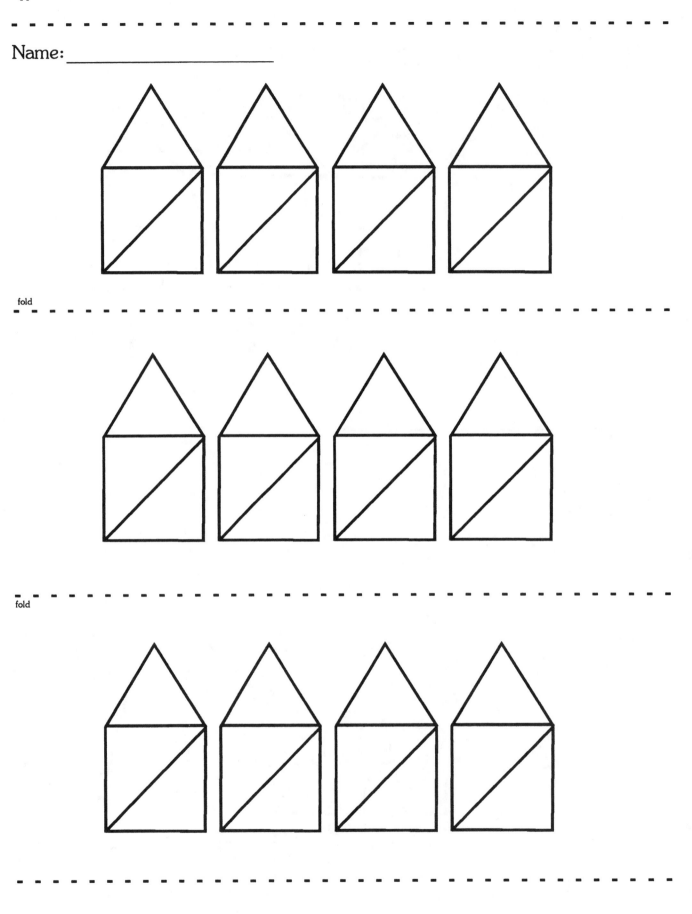

fold

fold

2.12. Sixth and Seventh Street practice houses

More Math, Please! Numbers over 10, © 2002 Zephyr Press, Tucson, AZ • 800-232-2187 • www.zephyrpress.com

2.13. Addition and subtraction practice, fives and sixes

Name: _____

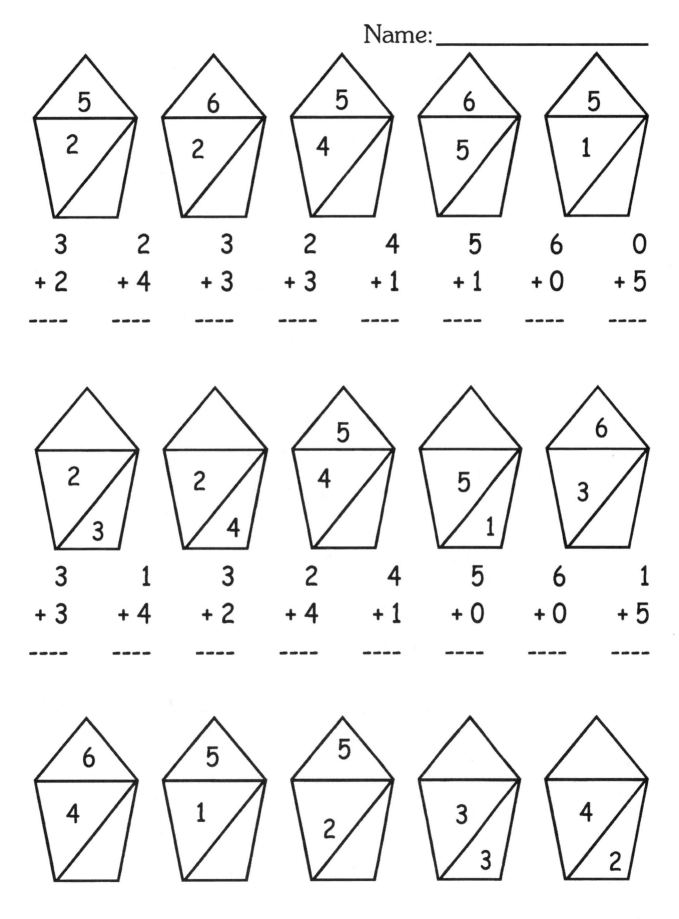

3	2	3	2	4	5	6	0
+ 2	+ 4	+ 3	+ 3	+ 1	+ 1	+ 0	+ 5
----	----	----	----	----	----	----	----

3	1	3	2	4	5	6	1
+ 3	+ 4	+ 2	+ 4	+ 1	+ 0	+ 0	+ 5
----	----	----	----	----	----	----	----

2.14. Addition and subtraction practice, threes to sixes

Name:_____

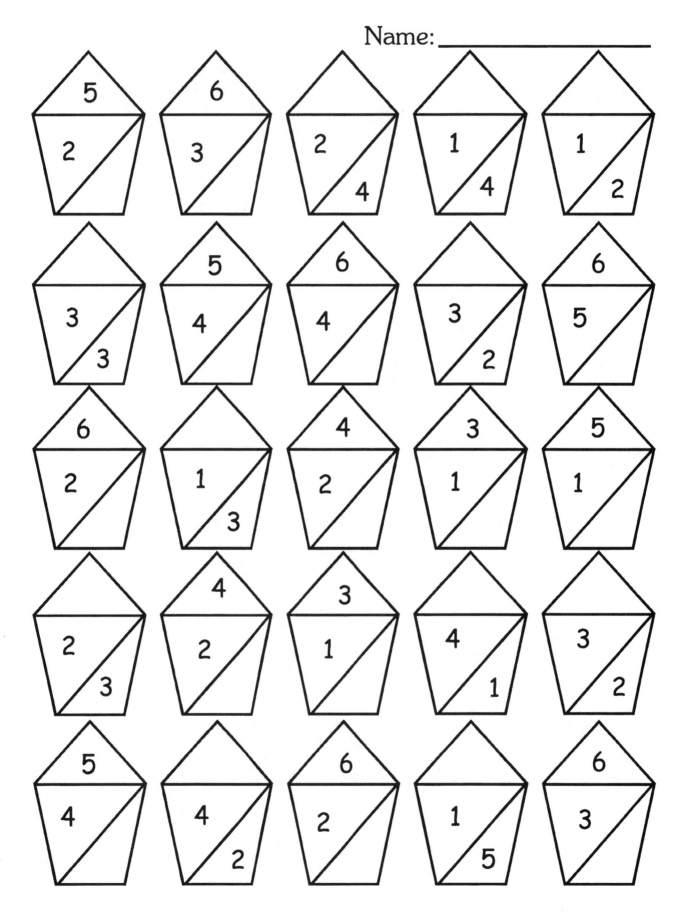

2.15a. Sevens

Figure out which families can live in each house.

0 1 2 3 4 5 6 7

Name: _____

. . . .

2.15b. Eights

Figure out which families can live in each house.

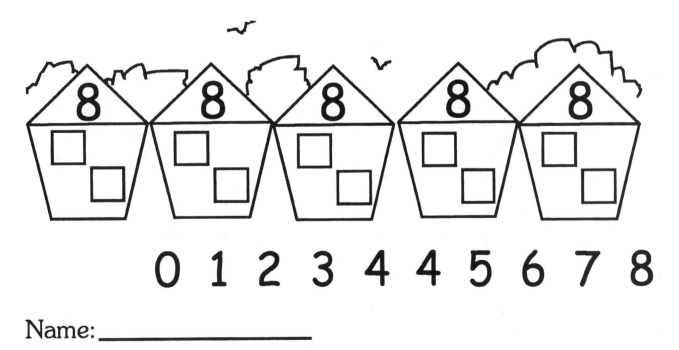

0 1 2 3 4 4 5 6 7 8

Name: _____

Name: _____

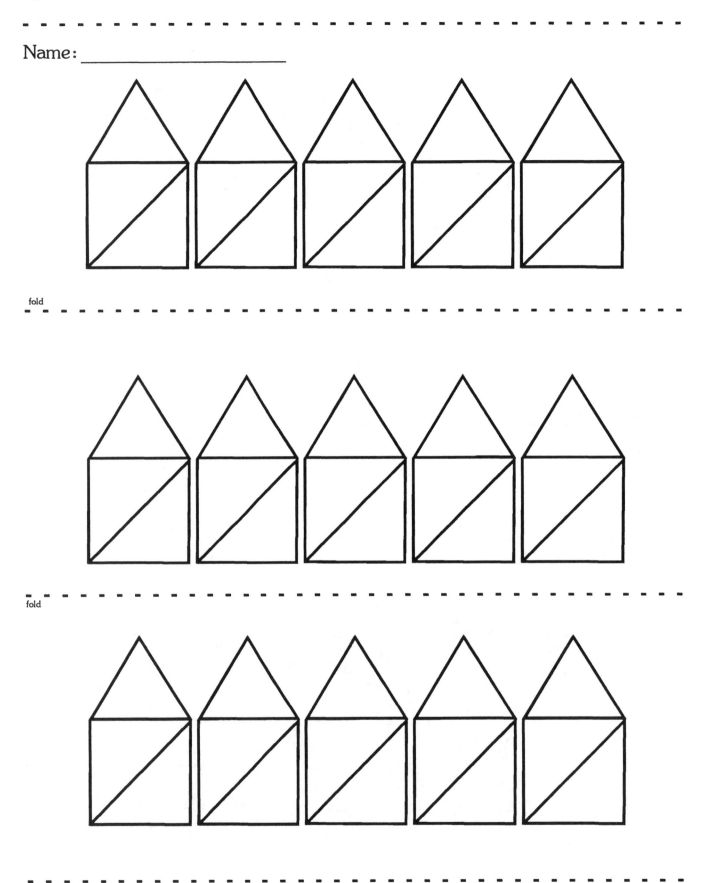

fold

fold

2.16. Eighth and Ninth Street practice houses

2.17. Addition and subtraction practice, sevens and eights

Name: _____

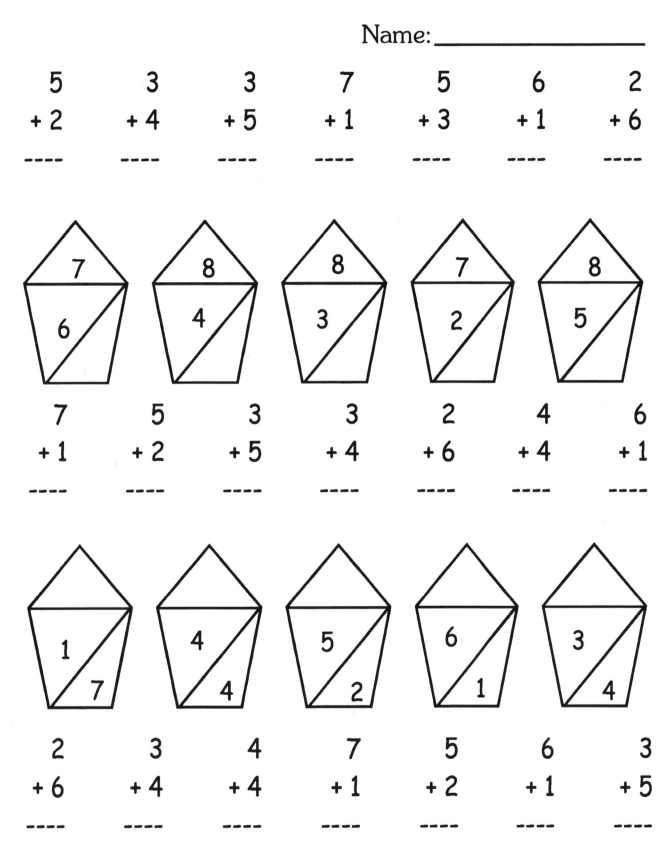

5	3	3	7	5	6	2
+ 2	+ 4	+ 5	+ 1	+ 3	+ 1	+ 6
----	----	----	----	----	----	----

7	5	3	3	2	4	6
+ 1	+ 2	+ 5	+ 4	+ 6	+ 4	+ 1
----	----	----	----	----	----	----

2	3	4	7	5	6	3
+ 6	+ 4	+ 4	+ 1	+ 2	+ 1	+ 5
----	----	----	----	----	----	----

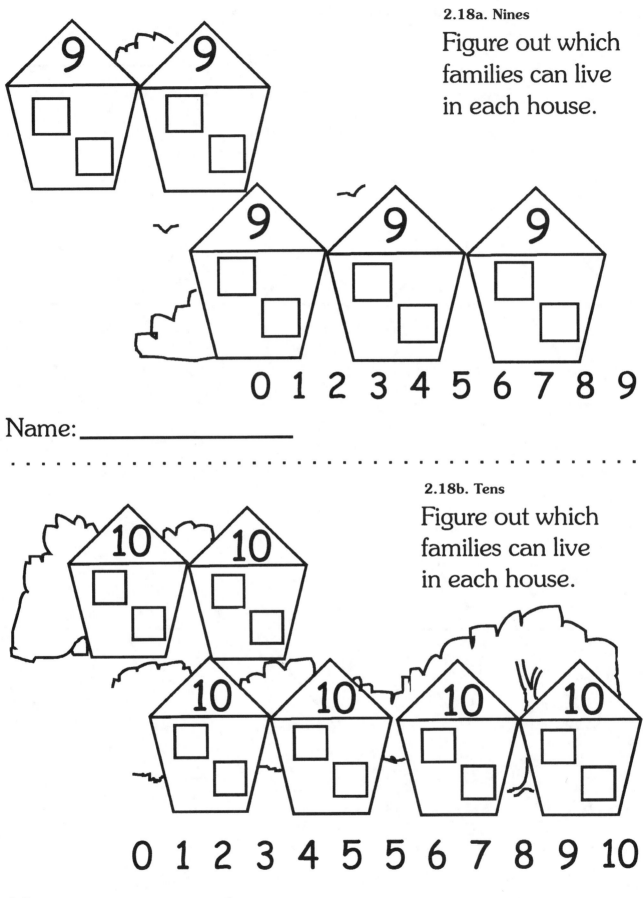

2.18a. Nines

Figure out which families can live in each house.

0 1 2 3 4 5 6 7 8 9

Name:_____

2.18b. Tens

Figure out which families can live in each house.

0 1 2 3 4 5 5 6 7 8 9 10

Name:_____

Name: _____

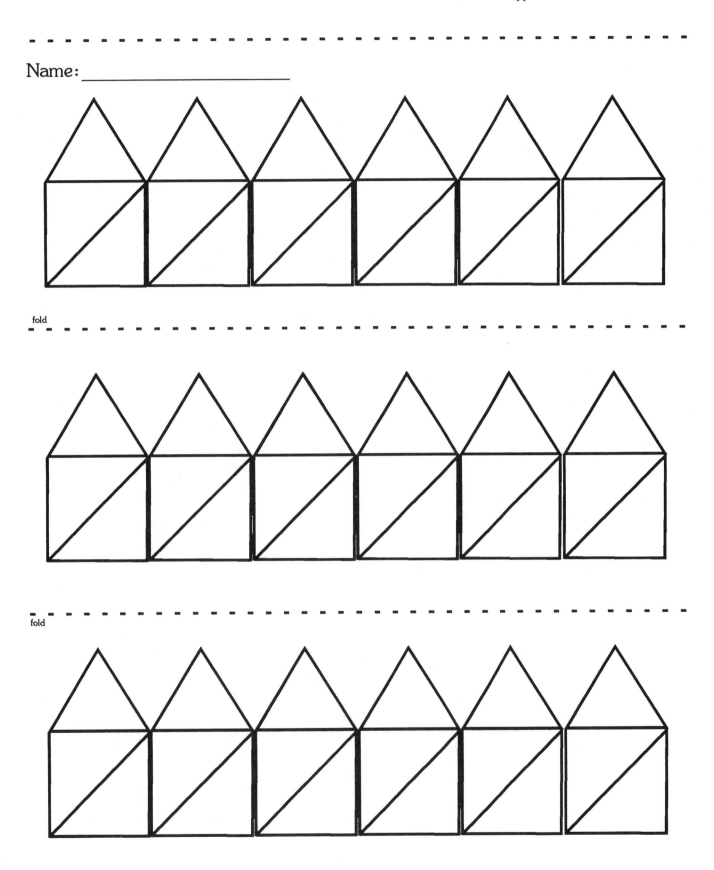

fold

fold

2.19. Tenth Street practice houses

2.20. Addition and subtraction practice, nines and tens

Name: _____

8	5	5	7	6	6	2
+ 2	+ 4	+ 5	+ 2	+ 3	+ 4	+ 7
----	----	----	----	----	----	----

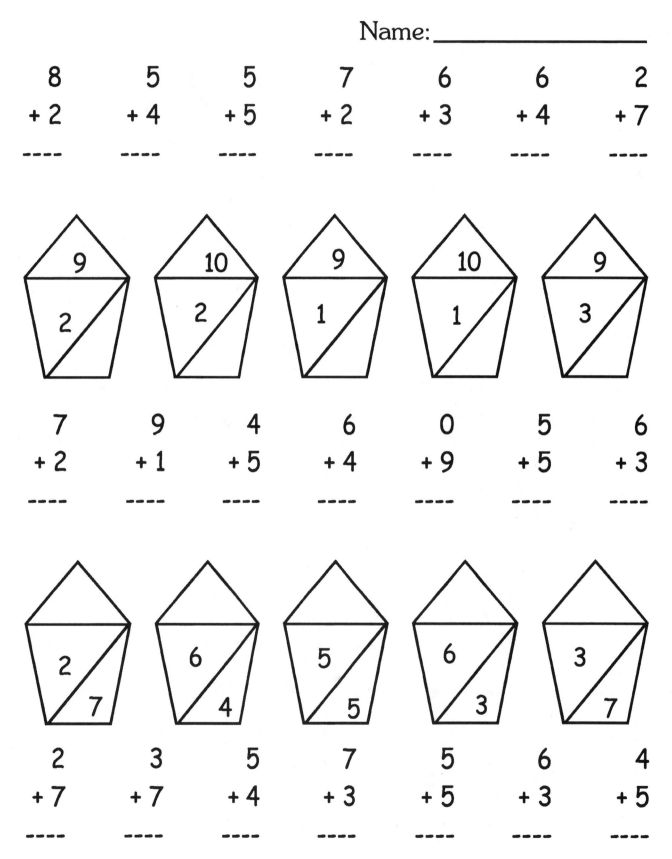

7	9	4	6	0	5	6
+ 2	+ 1	+ 5	+ 4	+ 9	+ 5	+ 3
----	----	----	----	----	----	----

2	3	5	7	5	6	4
+ 7	+ 7	+ 4	+ 3	+ 5	+ 3	+ 5
----	----	----	----	----	----	----

2.21. Addition and subtraction practice, sevens to tens

Name: _____

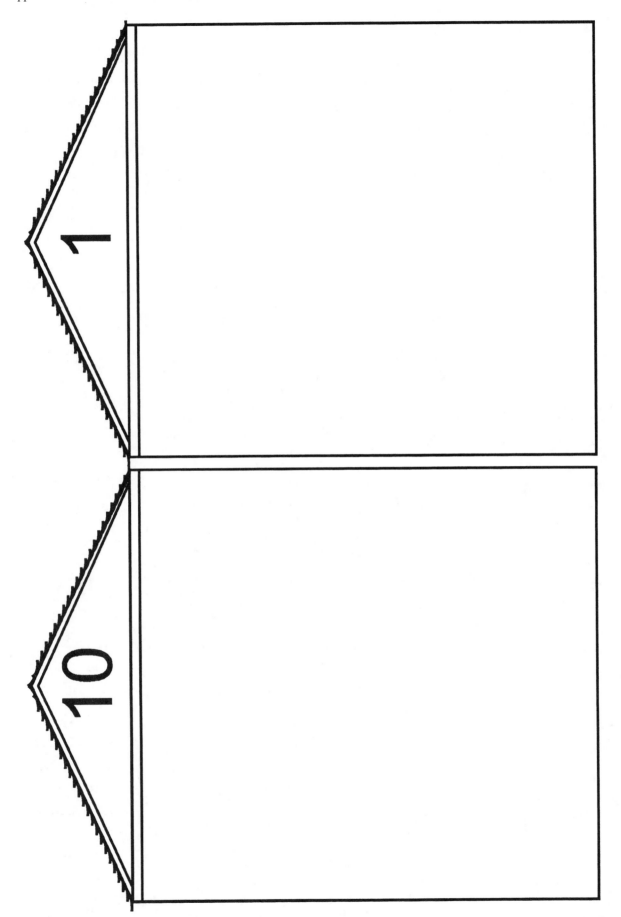

3.1. Place-value transparency

2 people want to rent an office	**3** people want to rent an office	**4** people want to rent an office
5 people want to rent an office	**6** people want to rent an office	**4** people want to rent an office
5 people want to rent an office	**4** people want to rent an office	**3** people want to rent an office
2 people want to rent an office	**2** people want to rent an office	**3** people want to rent an office

3.2. Rent-an-office game cards

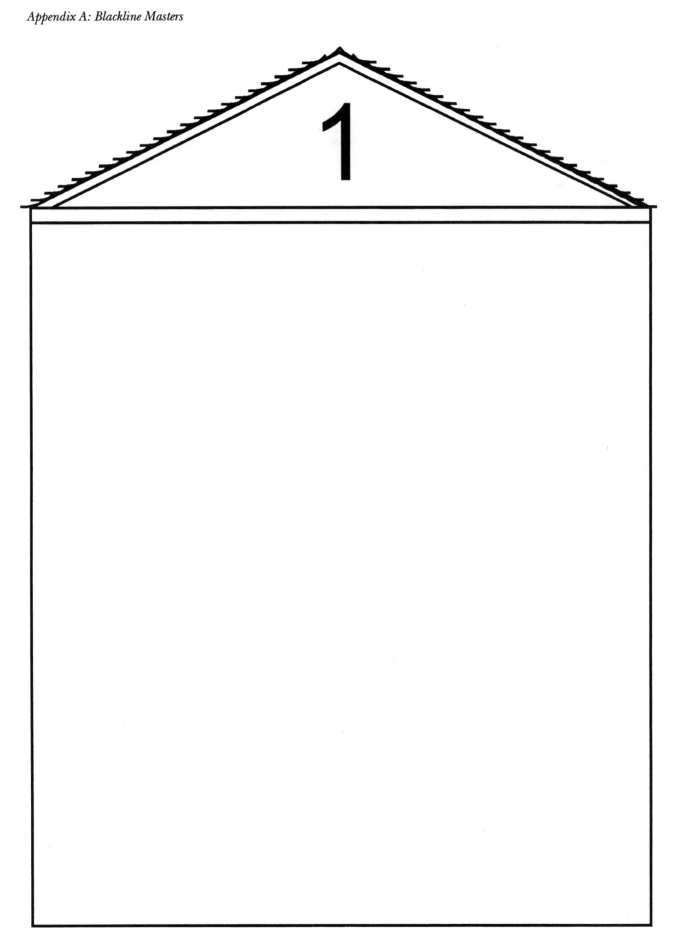

3.3a. Place-value mat 1

3.3b. Place-value mat 10

Name: _____

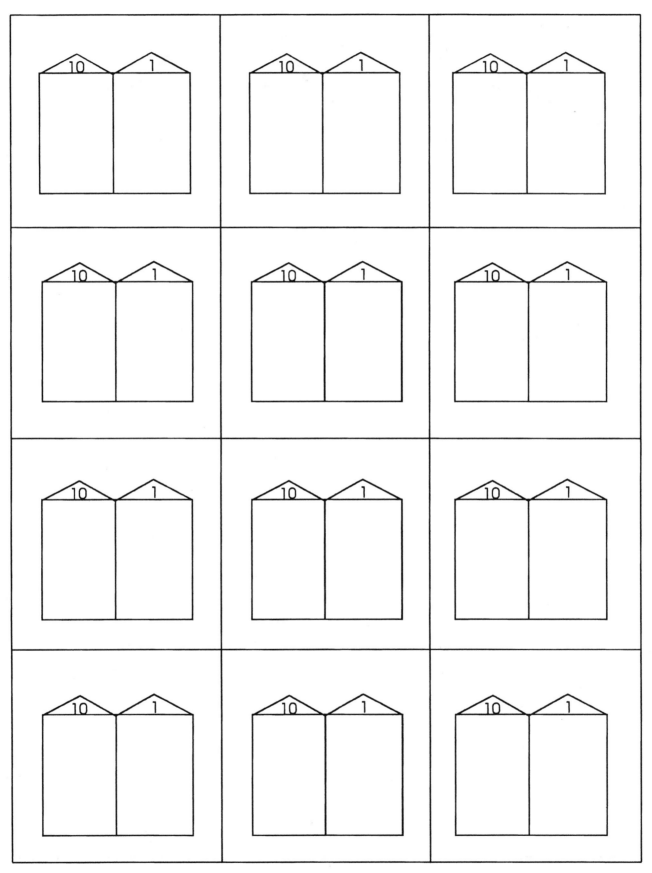

3.4. Blank place-value cards

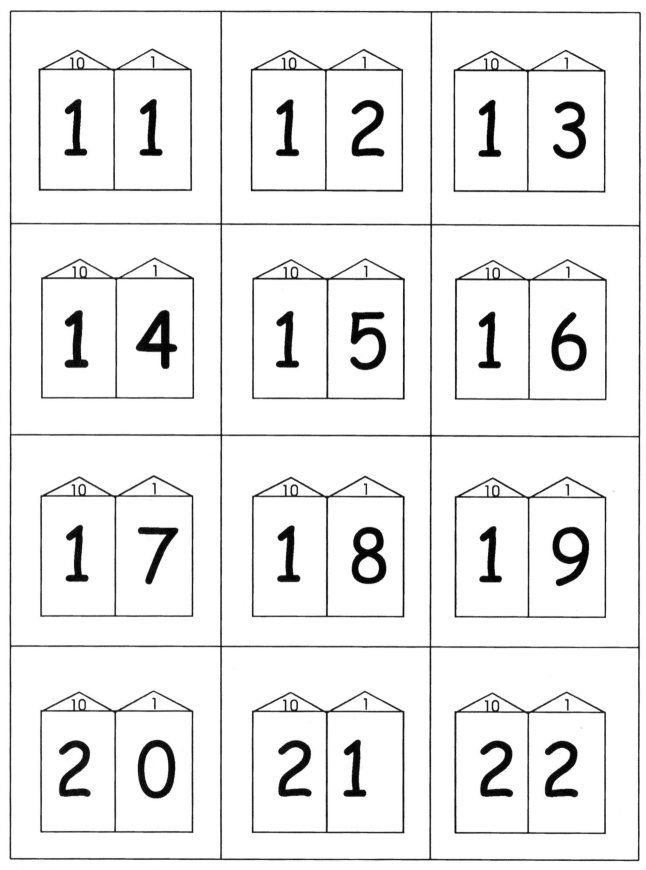

3.5a. Place-value cards, page 1

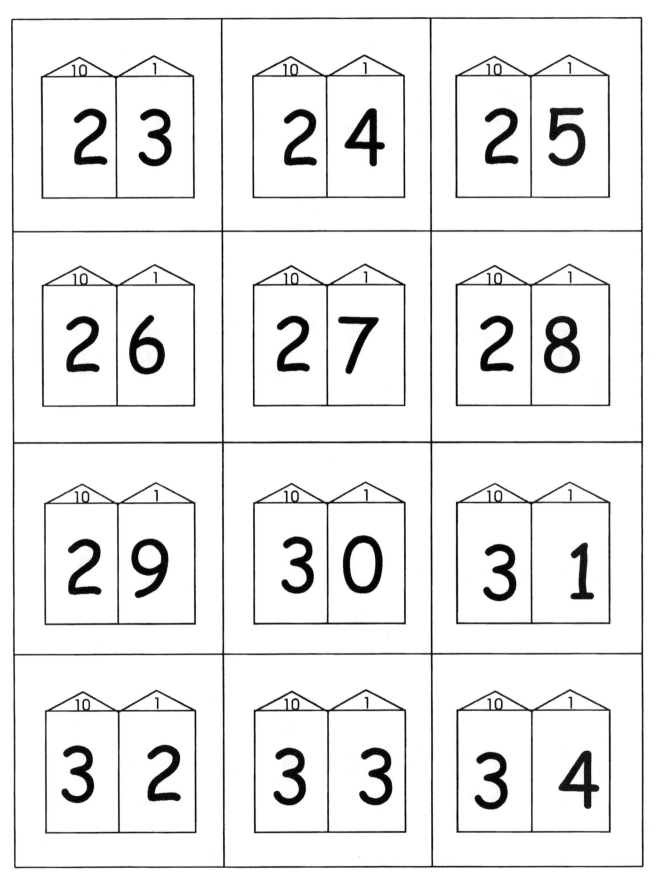

3.5b. Place-value cards, page 2

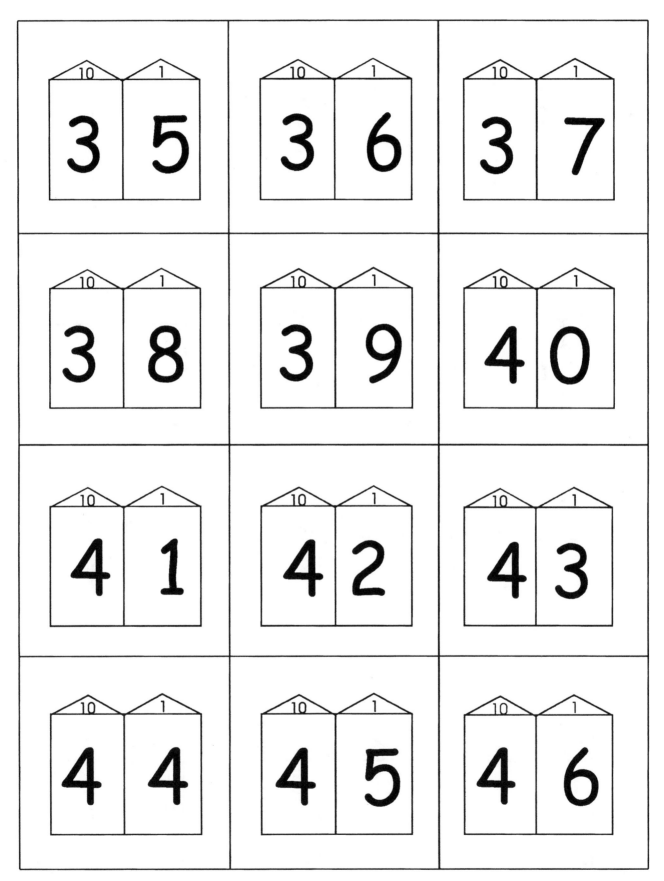

3.5c. Place-value cards, page 3

**When the teacher says a number,
write it in the 10 and 1 offices.
For example, if the teacher said
"twenty-three," you would write:**

Name: _____

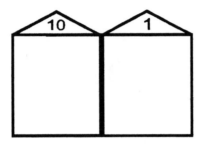
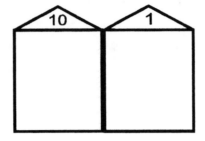
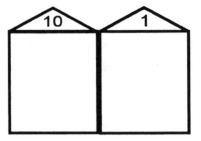

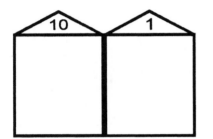
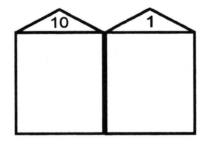
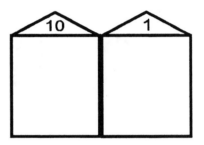

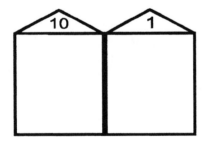
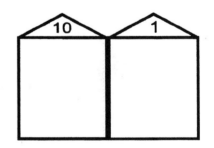

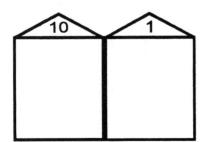
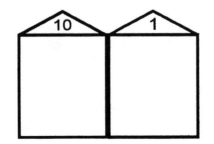
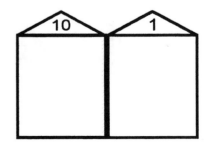

3.6. Give me a . . .

Write the number shown in each office on the line underneath it.

Name: _____

10	1	10	1	10	1
_____		_____		_____	

10	1	10	1	10	1
_____		_____		_____	

10	1	10	1	10	1
_____		_____		_____	

10	1	10	1	10	1
_____		_____		_____	

3.7. From sticks to numbers

Draw a picture to show each number.
The first one is done for you.

Name: _____

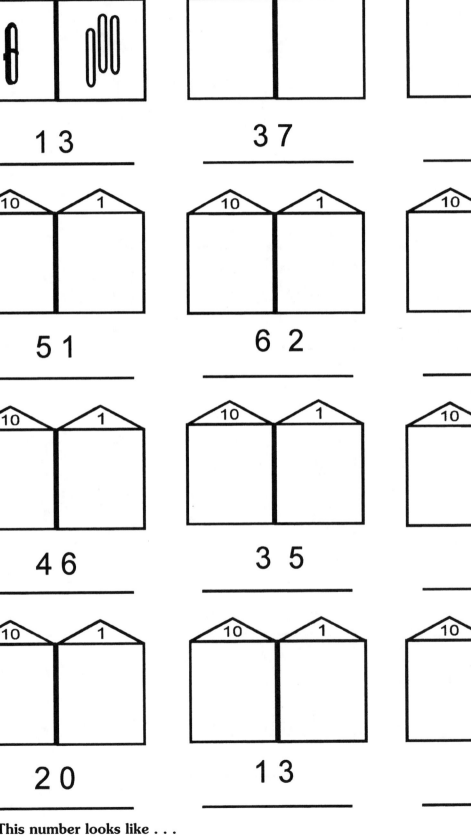

1 3

3 7

2 8

5 1

6 2

7 3

4 6

3 5

8 1

2 0

1 3

9

3.8. This number looks like . . .

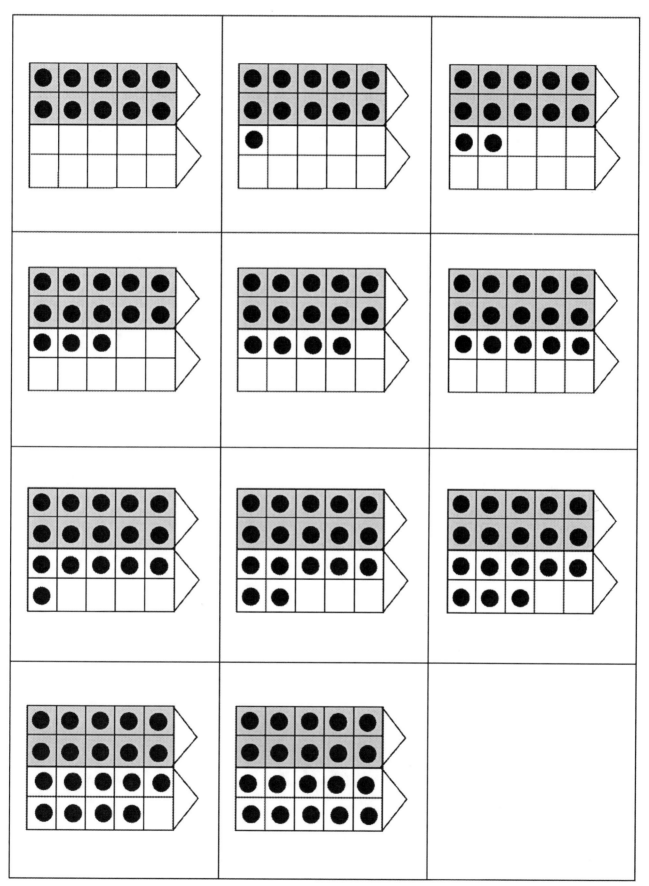

4.1. "Ten and more" dot cards

12   11   10

15   14   13

18   17   16

20   19

More Math, Please! Numbers over 10, © 2002 Zephyr Press, Tucson, AZ • 800-232-2187 • www.zephyrpress.com

10 + 2 ----	12 + 1 ----	11 + 2 ----
10 + 3 ----	13 + 1 ----	14 + 2 ----
15 + 3 ----	12 + 2 ----	11 + 3 ----
10 + 4 ----	14 + 1 ----	13 + 2 ----

4.2a. Ones-place addition cards, page 1

13   13   12

16   14   13

14   14   18

15   15   14

13 + 2 ----	12 + 3 ----	11 + 4 ----
10 + 5 ----	13 + 3 ----	12 + 4 ----
11 + 5 ----	10 + 6 ----	15 + 2 ----
14 + 3 ----	13 + 4 ----	12 + 5 ----

4.2b. Ones-place addition cards, page 2

15   15   15

16   16   15

17   16   16

17   17   17

11 + 6 ----	10 + 7 ----	17 + 1 ----
16 + 2 ----	15 + 3 ----	14 + 4 ----
13 + 3 ----	12 + 6 ----	11 + 7 ----
10 + 8 ----	13 + 6 ----	14 + 5 ----

4.2c. Ones-place addition cards, page 3

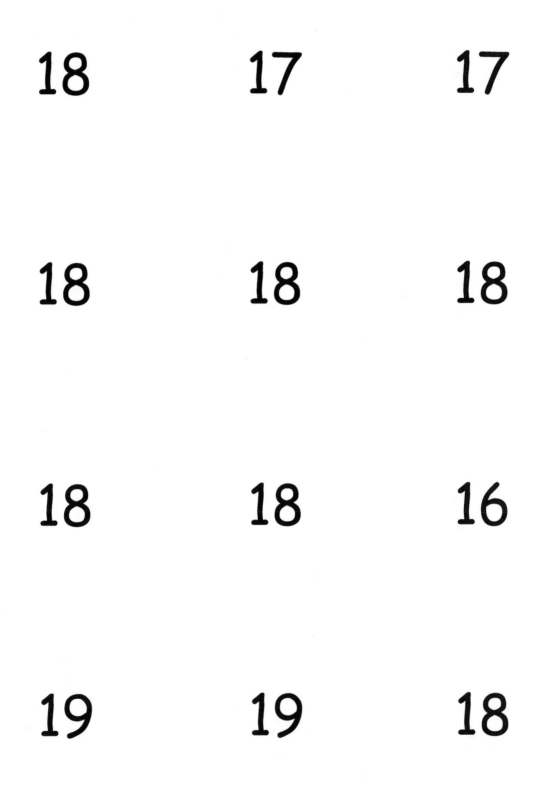

18	17	17
18	18	18
18	18	16
19	19	18

   More Math, Please! Numbers over 10, © 2002 Zephyr Press, Tucson, AZ • 800-232-2187 • www.zephyrpress.com

10 + 7 ----	11 + 6 ----	16 + 2 ----
15 + 3 ----	14 + 4 ----	13 + 5 ----
12 + 6 ----	11 + 7 ----	10 + 8 ----
17 + 2 ----	16 + 3 ----	15 + 4 ----

4.2d. Ones-place addition cards, page 4

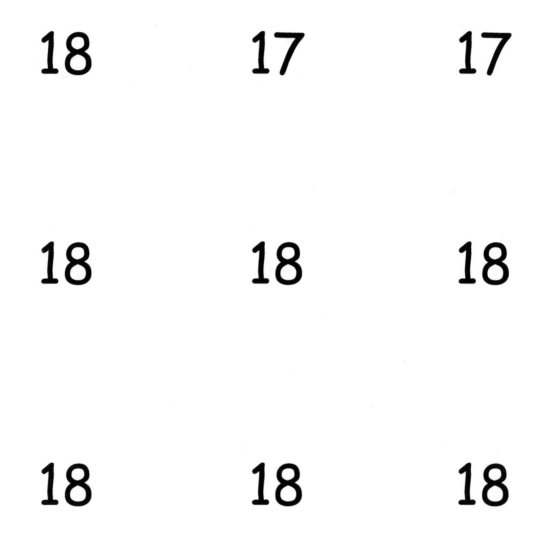

18	17	17
18	18	18
18	18	18
19	19	19

13	12	11
+ 6	+ 7	+ 8
----	----	----
10	18	11
+ 9	+ 1	+ 1
----	----	----
17	16	15
+ 1	+ 1	+ 1
----	----	----
14	13	12
+ 1	+ 1	+ 1
----	----	----

4.2e. Ones-place addition cards, page 5

19   19   19

12   19   19

16   17   18

13   14   15

19 - 1 ----	19 - 2 ----	19 - 3 ----
19 - 4 ----	19 - 5 ----	19 - 6 ----
19 - 7 ----	19 - 8 ----	19 - 9 ----

4.3a. Ones-place subtraction cards, page 1

16   17   18

13   14   15

10   11   12

17 - 4 ----	17 - 5 ----	17 - 6 ----
17 - 7 ----	18 - 1 ----	18 - 2 ----
18 - 3 ----	18 - 4 ----	18 - 5 ----
18 - 6 ----	18 - 7 ----	18 - 8 ----

4.3b. Ones-place subtraction cards, page 2

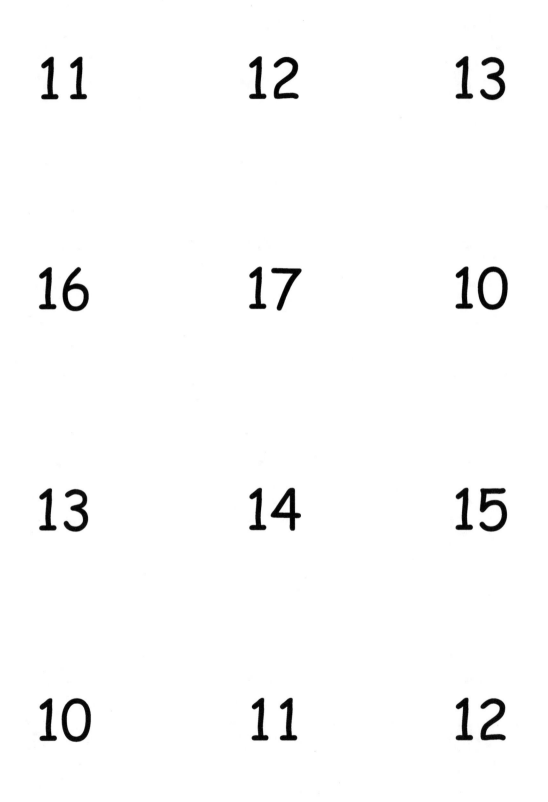

11	12	13
16	17	10
13	14	15
10	11	12

15 − 3 ----	15 − 4 ----	15 − 5 ----
16 − 1 ----	16 − 2 ----	16 − 3 ----
16 − 4 ----	16 − 5 ----	16 − 6 ----
17 − 1 ----	17 − 2 ----	17 − 3 ----

4.3c. Ones-place subtraction cards, page 3

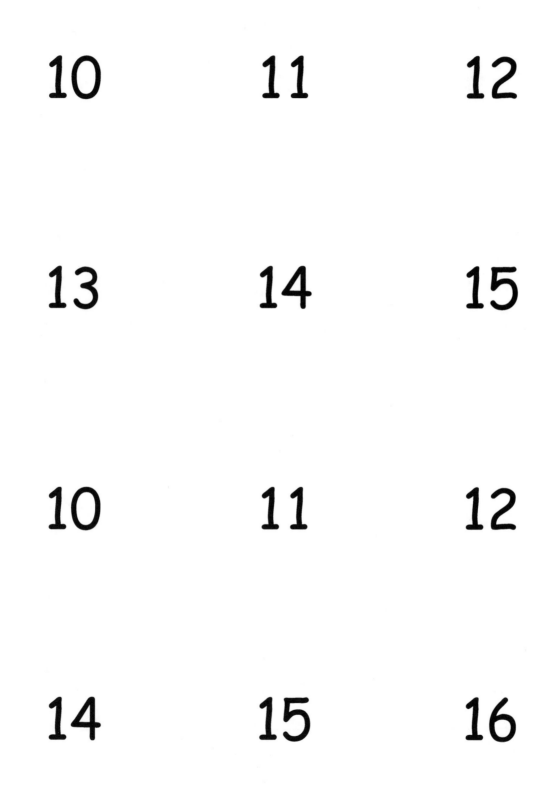

10 11 12

13 14 15

10 11 12

14 15 16

More Math, Please! Numbers over 10, © 2002 Zephyr Press, Tucson, AZ • 800-232-2187 • www.zephyrpress.com

11 – 1 ----	12 – 1 ----	12 – 2 ----
13 – 1 ----	13 – 2 ----	13 – 3 ----
14 – 1 ----	14 – 2 ----	14 – 3 ----
14 – 4 ----	15 – 1 ----	15 – 2 ----

4.3d. Ones-place subtraction cards, page 4

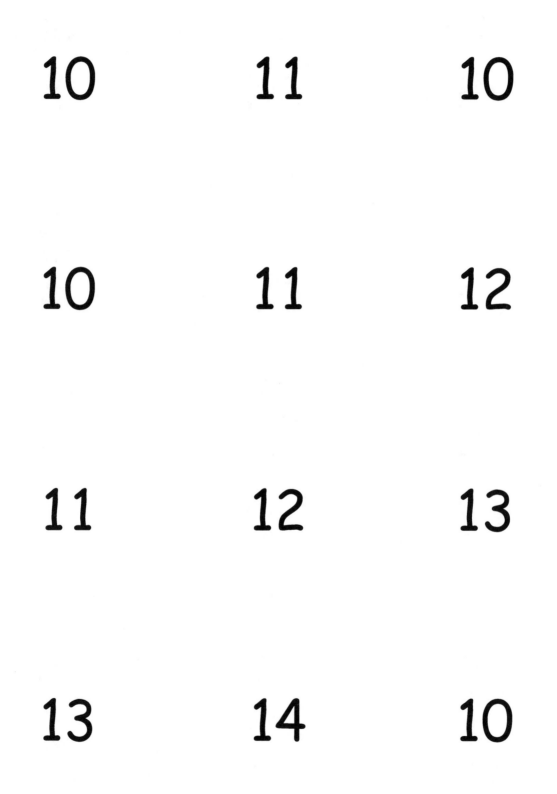

More Math, Please! Numbers over 10, © 2002 Zephyr Press, Tucson, AZ • 800-232-2187 • www.zephyrpress.com

2 + 9 - - - -	3 + 8 - - - -	4 + 7 - - - -
5 + 6 - - - -	3 + 9 - - - -	4 + 8 - - - -
5 + 7 - - - -	6 + 6 - - - -	4 + 9 - - - -
5 + 8 - - - -	6 + 7 - - - -	5 + 9 - - - -

4.4a. "Make a ten" addition cards, page 1

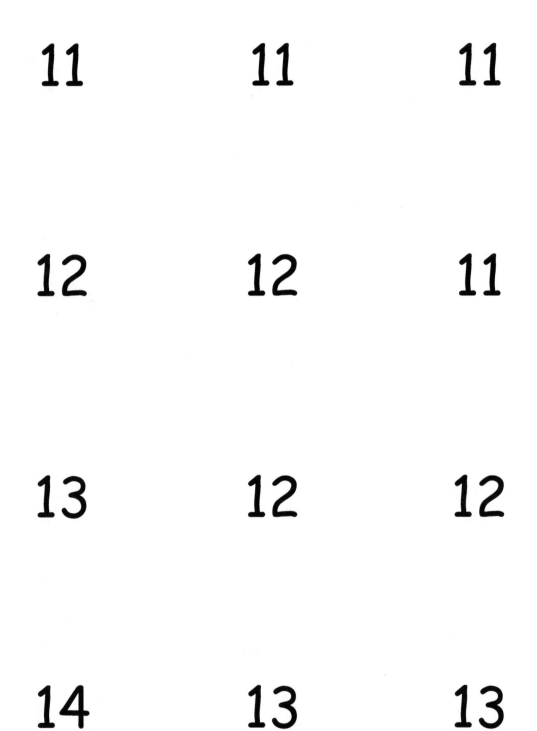

11	11	11
12	12	11
13	12	12
14	13	13

 More Math, Please! Numbers over 10, © 2002 Zephyr Press, Tucson, AZ • 800-232-2187 • www.zephyrpress.com

6 + 8 – – – –	7 + 7 – – – –	6 + 9 – – – –
7 + 8 – – – –	7 + 9 – – – –	8 + 8 – – – –
8 + 9 – – – –	9 + 9 – – – –	

4.4b. "Make a ten" addition cards, page 2

15   14   14

16   16   15

18   17

11 − 9 ----	11 − 8 ----	11 − 7 ----
11 − 6 ----	11 − 5 ----	11 − 4 ----
11 − 3 ----	11 − 2 ----	12 − 9 ----
12 − 8 ----	12 −7 ----	12 − 6 ----

4.5a. "Take from ten" subtraction cards, page 1

More Math, Please! Numbers over 10, © 2002 Zephyr Press, Tucson, AZ • 800-232-2187 • www.zephyrpress.com

12 - 5 ----	12 - 4 ----	12 - 3 ----
13 - 9 ----	13 - 8 ----	13 - 7 ----
13 - 6 ----	13 - 5 ----	13 - 4 ----
14 - 9 ----	14 - 8 ----	14 - 7 ----

4.5b. "Take from ten" subtraction cards, page 2

14 - 6 ----	14 - 5 ----	15 - 9 ----
15 - 8 ----	15 - 7 ----	15 - 6 ----
16 - 9 ----	16 - 8 ----	16 - 7 ----
17 - 9 ----	17 - 8 ----	18 - 9 ----

4.5c. "Take from ten" subtraction cards, page 3

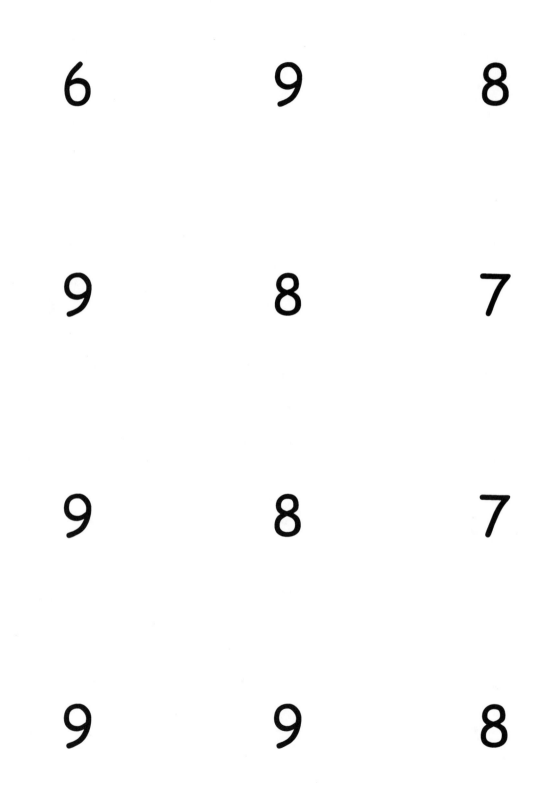

+10	+11	+12
+13	+14	+15
+16	+17	+18
+19	+20	+21

4.6a. Double-digit addition cards, page 1

+22	+23	+24
+25	+26	+27
+28	+29	+30
+31	+32	+33

4.6b. Double-digit addition cards, page 2

-10	-11	-12
-13	-14	-15
-16	-17	-18
-19	-20	-21

4.7a. Double-digit subtraction cards, page 1

-22	-23	-24
-25	-26	-27
-28	-29	-30
-31	-32	-33

4.7b. Double-digit subtraction cards, page 2

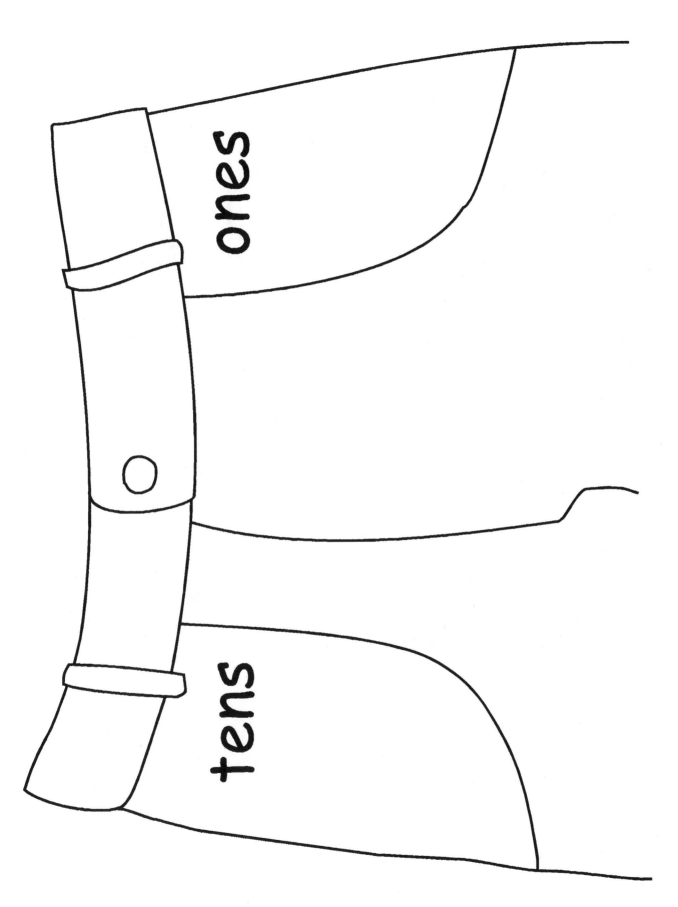

4.8. Moneybags

Name: _____

4.9a. Assessment worksheet 1

   More Math, Please! Numbers over 10, © 2002 Zephyr Press, Tucson, AZ • 800-232-2187 • www.zephyrpress.com

Name: _____

4.9b. Assessment worksheet 2

Name: _____

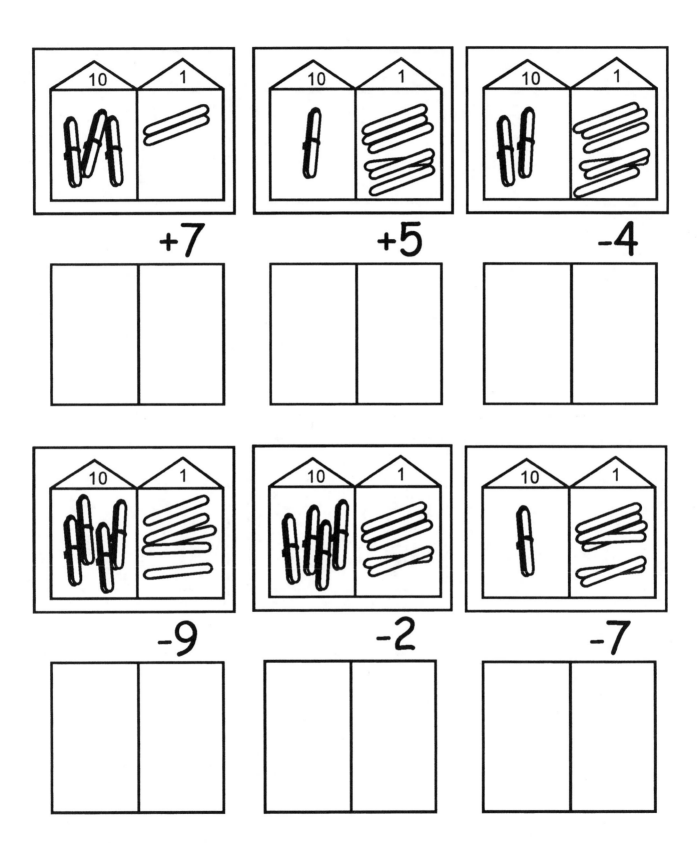

4.9c. Assessment worksheet 3

   More Math, Please! Numbers over 10, © 2002 Zephyr Press, Tucson, AZ • 800-232-2187 • www.zephyrpress.com

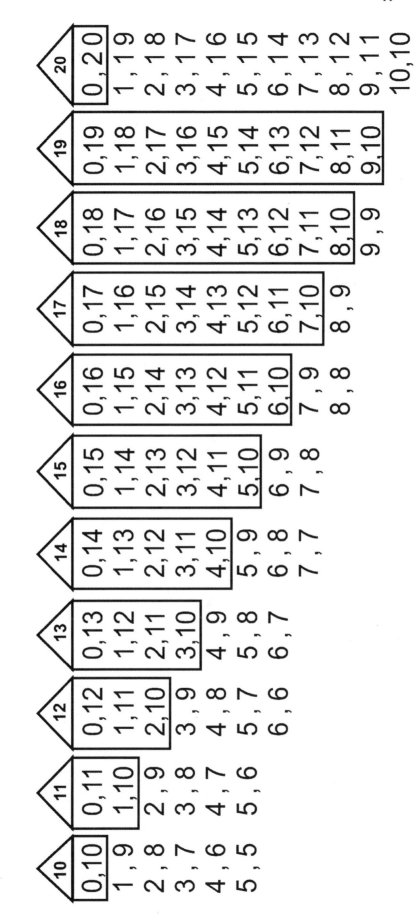

5.1. Computation to 20: a global view

Name: _____

11	18	13	16	14
+ 7	+ 1	+ 6	+ 3	+ 2
-----	-----	-----	-----	-----

10	12	12	15	13
+ 8	+ 6	+ 5	+ 4	+ 3
-----	-----	-----	-----	-----

17	16	12	14	13
+ 2	+ 3	+ 6	+ 3	+ 5
-----	-----	-----	-----	-----

16	12	13	13	14
+ 3	+ 4	+ 6	+ 5	+ 4
-----	-----	-----	-----	-----

15	14	17	12	13
+ 4	+ 3	+ 2	+ 5	+ 2
-----	-----	-----	-----	-----

5.2a. Adding ones, page 1

 More Math, Please! Numbers over 10, © 2002 Zephyr Press, Tucson, AZ • 800-232-2187 • www.zephyrpress.com

Name: _____

12 + 3 -----	11 + 5 -----	12 + 5 -----	13 + 1 -----	14 + 1 -----
11 + 4 -----	10 + 6 -----	10 + 2 -----	14 + 2 -----	13 + 2 -----
10 + 5 -----	15 + 2 -----	12 + 1 -----	15 + 3 -----	10 + 7 -----
13 + 3 -----	14 + 3 -----	11 + 2 -----	11 + 3 -----	15 + 3 -----
12 + 4 -----	13 + 4 -----	10 + 3 -----	10 + 4 -----	12 + 6 -----

5.2b. Adding ones, page 2

Name: _____

13	12	13	16	11
+ 6	+ 3	+ 1	+ 2	+ 7
-----	-----	-----	-----	-----
12	17	12	15	10
+ 7	+ 1	+ 1	+ 3	+ 8
-----	-----	-----	-----	-----
11	16	11	14	13
+ 8	+ 1	+ 6	+ 4	+ 6
-----	-----	-----	-----	-----
10	15	10	13	14
+ 9	+ 1	+ 7	+ 3	+ 5
-----	-----	-----	-----	-----
18	14	17	12	13
+ 1	+ 1	+ 1	+ 6	+ 2
-----	-----	-----	-----	-----

5.2c. Adding ones, page 3

More Math, Please! Numbers over 10, © 2002 Zephyr Press, Tucson, AZ • 800-232-2187 • www.zephyrpress.com

Name: _____

11	15	16	12	14
- 1	- 1	- 5	- 2	- 4
-----	-----	-----	-----	-----

13	14	11	13	14
- 3	- 2	- 0	- 1	- 3
-----	-----	-----	-----	-----

14	13	15	14	12
- 1	- 2	- 2	- 2	- 1
-----	-----	-----	-----	-----

16	16	15	13	14
- 4	- 6	- 3	- 0	- 4
-----	-----	-----	-----	-----

15	16	16	15	13
- 4	- 3	- 2	- 5	- 0
-----	-----	-----	-----	-----

5.3a. Taking from ones, page 1

Name: _____

17	19	18	19	19
- 7	- 1	- 8	- 2	- 5
-----	-----	-----	-----	-----

18	19	17	18	17
- 7	- 3	- 5	- 6	- 6
-----	-----	-----	-----	-----

17	18	19	17	18
- 3	- 5	- 4	- 4	- 1
-----	-----	-----	-----	-----

17	19	18	19	17
- 1	- 7	- 3	- 6	- 2
-----	-----	-----	-----	-----

18	19	19	19	18
- 4	- 8	- 0	- 9	- 2
-----	-----	-----	-----	-----

5.3b. Taking from ones, page 2

More Math, Please! Numbers over 10, © 2002 Zephyr Press, Tucson, AZ • 800-232-2187 • www.zephyrpress.com

Name: _____

11	19	13	16	14
- 1	- 7	- 2	- 3	-2
-----	-----	-----	-----	-----
18	12	15	15	13
- 5	- 2	- 3	- 4	- 3
-----	-----	-----	-----	-----
17	16	19	14	18
- 2	- 5	- 6	-3	- 6
-----	-----	-----	-----	-----
16	19	18	17	18
- 5	- 4	- 6	- 5	- 7
-----	-----	-----	-----	-----
17	18	17	18	19
- 3	- 4	- 4	- 3	- 2
-----	-----	-----	-----	-----

5.3c. Taking from ones, page 3

Name: _____

9 + 2 -----	9 + 7 -----	9 + 9 -----	4 + 9 -----	8 + 9 -----
3 + 9 -----	6 + 9 -----	5 + 9 -----	9 + 3 -----	9 + 2 -----
9 + 8 -----	9 + 4 -----	9 + 5 -----	9 + 6 -----	7 + 9 -----
9 + 2 -----	9 + 3 -----	9 + 9 -----	5 + 9 -----	9 + 6 -----
4 + 9 -----	9 + 7 -----	9 + 5 -----	9 + 3 -----	6 + 9 -----

6.1. Nines "make a ten" problems

More Math, Please! Numbers over 10, © 2002 Zephyr Press, Tucson, AZ • 800-232-2187 • www.zephyrpress.com

Name: _____

8 + 7 -----	8 + 3 -----	8 + 4 -----	5 + 8 -----	8 + 7 -----
6 + 8 -----	8 + 4 -----	8 + 5 -----	8 + 8 -----	6 + 8 -----

6.2. Eights "make a ten" problems

- -

Name: _____

7 + 8 -----	3 + 8 -----	8 + 5 -----	4 + 7 -----	8 + 8 -----
7 + 7 -----	5 + 7 -----	6 + 7 -----	4 + 8 -----	8 + 6 -----

6.3. Sevens and eights "make a ten" problems

More Math, Please! Numbers over 10, © 2002 Zephyr Press, Tucson, AZ • 800-232-2187 • www.zephyrpress.com

Name: _____

9 + 2 -----	9 + 7 -----	9 + 9 -----	4 + 9 -----	8 + 9 -----
9 + 3 -----	2 + 9 -----	8 + 9 -----	3 + 9 -----	7 + 9 -----
4 + 9 -----	9 + 6 -----	9 + 7 -----	8 + 4 -----	8 + 5 -----
9 + 5 -----	8 + 3 -----	8 + 4 -----	5 + 8 -----	8 + 7 -----
6 + 9 -----	8 + 4 -----	8 + 5 -----	8 + 3 -----	6 + 8 -----

6.4. Eights and nines "make a ten" problems

More Math, Please! Numbers over 10, © 2002 Zephyr Press, Tucson, AZ • 800-232-2187 • www.zephyrpress.com

Name: _____

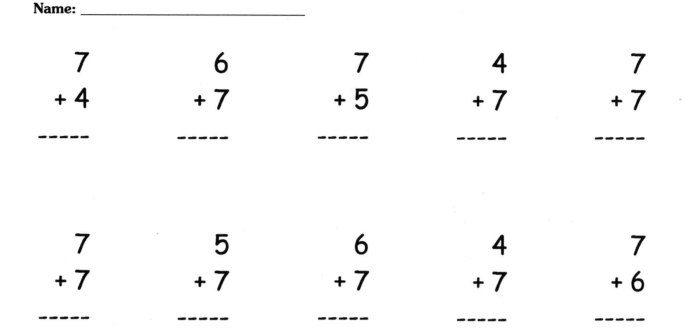

7	6	7	4	7
+ 4	+ 7	+ 5	+ 7	+ 7
-----	-----	-----	-----	-----

7	5	6	4	7
+ 7	+ 7	+ 7	+ 7	+ 6
-----	-----	-----	-----	-----

6.5. Sevens "make a ten" problems

_____

Name: _____

5	6	6	6	6
+ 6	+ 6	+ 5	+ 6	+ 4
-----	-----	-----	-----	-----

6.6. Sixes "make a ten" problems

Name: _____

9 + 7 -----	4 + 8 -----	9 + 9 -----	8 + 8 -----	9 + 2 -----
2 + 9 -----	3 + 8 -----	8 + 9 -----	7 + 9 -----	3 + 9 -----
9 + 6 -----	7 + 4 -----	8 + 7 -----	7 + 5 -----	4 + 9 -----
9 + 3 -----	5 + 7 -----	8 + 6 -----	7 + 6 -----	9 + 5 -----
9 + 4 -----	7 + 7 -----	8 + 5 -----	6 + 9 -----	6 + 9 -----

6.7. Sevens, eights, and nines "make a ten" problems

More Math, Please! Numbers over 10, © 2002 Zephyr Press, Tucson, AZ • 800-232-2187 • www.zephyrpress.com

Name: _____

9	8	9	9	4
+ 9	+ 7	+ 7	+ 2	+ 8
-----	-----	-----	-----	-----

8	7	8	3	3
+ 9	+ 9	+ 8	+ 9	+ 8
-----	-----	-----	-----	-----

8	6	9	4	7
+ 7	+ 5	+ 6	+ 9	+ 4
-----	-----	-----	-----	-----

8	7	9	9	5
+ 6	+ 6	+ 3	+ 5	+ 7
-----	-----	-----	-----	-----

8	6	9	6	7
+ 5	+ 9	+ 4	+ 9	+ 6
-----	-----	-----	-----	-----

6.8a. Sixes–nines "make a ten" problems, page 1

Name: _____

9	9	9	4	8
+ 2	+ 7	+ 9	+ 8	+ 7
-----	-----	-----	-----	-----

3	2	8	3	7
+ 9	+ 9	+ 9	+ 8	+ 9
-----	-----	-----	-----	-----

4	9	8	7	6
+ 9	+ 6	+ 7	+ 4	+ 5
-----	-----	-----	-----	-----

9	9	8	5	7
+ 5	+ 3	+ 6	+ 7	+ 6
-----	-----	-----	-----	-----

6	9	8	7	6
+ 9	+ 4	+ 5	+ 6	+ 6
-----	-----	-----	-----	-----

6.8b. Sixes to nines "make a ten" problems, page 2

More Math, Please! Numbers over 10, © 2002 Zephyr Press, Tucson, AZ • 800-232-2187 • www.zephyrpress.com

Name: _____

11 - 9 -----	14 - 9 -----	12 - 9 -----	15 - 9 -----
18 - 9 -----	16 - 9 -----	13 - 9 -----	18 - 9 -----
15 - 9 -----	17 - 9 -----	11 - 9 -----	12 - 9 -----
13 - 9 -----	18 - 9 -----	14 - 9 -----	16 - 9 -----
12 - 9 -----	15 - 9 -----	16 - 9 -----	11 - 9 -----

7.1. Nines "take from ten" problems

Name: _____

11 - 8 -----	14 - 8 -----	12 - 8 -----	15 - 8 -----
14 - 8 -----	16 - 8 -----	13 - 8 -----	10 - 8 -----
15 - 8 -----	17 - 8 -----	11 - 8 -----	12 - 8 -----
13 - 8 -----	10 - 8 -----	14 - 8 -----	16 - 8 -----
12 - 8 -----	15 - 8 -----	16 - 8 -----	11 - 8 -----

7.2. Eights "take from ten" problems

More Math, Please! Numbers over 10, © 2002 Zephyr Press, Tucson, AZ • 800-232-2187 • www.zephyrpress.com

Name: _____

11 - 8 -----	11 - 9 -----	14 - 8 -----	14 - 9 -----
12 - 9 -----	18 - 9 -----	16 - 8 -----	16 - 9 -----
15 - 8 -----	15 - 9 -----	17 - 8 -----	17 - 9 -----
13 - 8 -----	13 - 9 -----	14 - 8 -----	18 - 9 -----
12 - 8 -----	12 - 9 -----	15 - 8 -----	15 - 9 -----

7.3. Eights and nines "take from ten" problems

Name: _____

11 - 7 -----	14 - 7 -----	12 - 7 -----	15 - 7 -----
16 - 7 -----	16 - 7 -----	13 - 7 -----	10 - 7 -----
15 - 7 -----	13 - 7 -----	11 - 7 -----	12 - 7 -----
13 - 7 -----	10 - 7 -----	14 - 7 -----	16 - 7 -----
12 - 7 -----	15 - 7 -----	16 - 7 -----	11 - 7 -----

7.4. Sevens "take from ten" problems

More Math, Please! Numbers over 10, © 2002 Zephyr Press, Tucson, AZ • 800-232-2187 • www.zephyrpress.com

Name: _____

11 - 8 -----	14 - 7 -----	14 - 8 -----	15 - 7 -----
11 - 8 -----	16 - 7 -----	16 - 8 -----	10 - 7 -----
15 - 8 -----	12 - 7 -----	17 - 8 -----	12 - 7 -----
13 - 8 -----	13 - 7 -----	14 - 8 -----	14 - 7 -----
12 - 8 -----	15 - 7 -----	15 - 8 -----	11 - 7 -----

7.5. Sevens and eights "take from ten" problems

Name: _____

11	14	11	14	14	15
- 8	- 7	- 9	- 8	- 9	- 7
-----	-----	-----	-----	-----	-----
12	16	18	16	16	12
- 9	- 7	- 9	- 8	- 9	- 8
-----	-----	-----	-----	-----	-----
15	12	15	17	17	12
- 8	- 7	- 9	- 8	- 9	- 7
-----	-----	-----	-----	-----	-----
13	13	13	14	18	16
- 8	- 7	- 9	- 8	- 9	- 7
-----	-----	-----	-----	-----	-----
12	15	12	15	15	11
- 8	- 7	- 9	- 8	- 9	- 7
-----	-----	-----	-----	-----	-----

7.6. Sevens–nines "take from ten" problems

More Math, Please! Numbers over 10, © 2002 Zephyr Press, Tucson, AZ • 800-232-2187 • www.zephyrpress.com

Name: _____

11 - 6 -----	14 - 6 -----	12 - 6 -----	15 - 6 -----
10 - 6 -----	14 - 6 -----	13 - 6 -----	11 - 6 -----
15 - 6 -----	16 - 6 -----	11 - 6 -----	12 - 6 -----
13 - 6 -----	10 - 6 -----	14 - 6 -----	13 - 6 -----
12 - 6 -----	15 - 6 -----	10 - 6 -----	11 - 6 -----

7.7. Sixes "take from ten" problems

Name: _____

11 - 5 -----	14 - 5 -----	12 - 5 -----	13 - 4 -----
13 - 5 -----	11 - 4 -----	13 - 4 -----	12 - 4 -----
11 - 2 -----	12 - 3 -----	11 - 3 -----	12 - 3 -----
13 - 5 -----	14 - 5 -----	13 - 5 -----	12 - 5 -----
14 - 5 -----	13 - 4 -----	12 - 4 -----	11 - 4 -----

7.8. Twos–fives "take from ten" problems

More Math, Please! Numbers over 10, © 2002 Zephyr Press, Tucson, AZ • 800-232-2187 • www.zephyrpress.com

Name: _____

15 - 6 -----	14 - 5 -----	15 - 9 -----	14 - 7 -----	14 - 9 -----
14 - 6 -----	11 - 4 -----	18 - 9 -----	16 - 7 -----	16 - 9 -----
12 - 6 -----	11 - 3 -----	12 - 9 -----	17 - 8 -----	17 - 9 -----
16 - 8 -----	14 - 5 -----	16 - 9 -----	14 - 7 -----	18 - 9 -----
11 - 6 -----	13 - 4 -----	11 - 9 -----	15 - 7 -----	15 - 9 -----

7.9a. Mixed "take from ten" practice, page 1

Name: _____

14 - 6 -----	15 - 8 -----	11 - 9 -----	11 - 5 -----	15 - 7 -----
15 - 6 -----	16 - 8 -----	18 - 9 -----	13 - 5 -----	12 - 5 -----
17 - 8 -----	12 - 8 -----	15 - 9 -----	11 - 2 -----	12 - 7 -----
14 - 6 -----	16 - 8 -----	13 - 9 -----	13 - 5 -----	16 - 7 -----
15 - 6 -----	11 - 8 -----	12 - 9 -----	14 - 5 -----	11 - 7 -----

7.9b. Mixed "take from ten" practice, page 2

More Math, Please! Numbers over 10, © 2002 Zephyr Press, Tucson, AZ • 800-232-2187 • www.zephyrpress.com

Name: _____

11 - 6 -----	14 - 8 -----	12 - 8 -----	15 - 9 -----	12 - 5 -----
14 - 6 -----	16 - 8 -----	13 - 7 -----	17 - 9 -----	13 - 4 -----
15 - 6 -----	17 - 8 -----	11 - 8 -----	13 - 9 -----	11 - 3 -----
13 - 6 -----	18 - 9 -----	14 - 8 -----	14 - 9 -----	13 - 5 -----
12 - 6 -----	15 - 8 -----	16 - 8 -----	16 - 9 -----	12 - 4 -----

7.9c. Mixed "take from ten" practice, page 3

Name: _____

11 - 8 -----	12 - 6 -----	13 - 4 -----	12 -7 -----	11 -7 -----
18 - 9 -----	13 - 6 -----	12 - 4 -----	13 -7 -----	16 -7 -----
15 - 8 -----	11 - 6 -----	12 - 3 -----	11 -7 -----	15 -7 -----
13 - 8 -----	14 - 6 -----	12 - 5 -----	14 -7 -----	13 -7 -----
12 - 8 -----	16 -7 -----	11 - 4 -----	16 -7 -----	12 -7 -----

7.9d. Mixed "take from ten" practice, page 4

 More Math, Please! Numbers over 10, © 2002 Zephyr Press, Tucson, AZ • 800-232-2187 • www.zephyrpress.com

Name: _____

11 − 1 -----	18 + 1 -----	13 − 2 -----	13 + 1 -----	14 − 2 -----
18 − 5 -----	12 + 6 -----	15 − 3 -----	14 + 2 -----	13 − 3 -----
17 − 2 -----	16 + 3 -----	19 − 6 -----	15 + 3 -----	18 − 6 -----
16 − 5 -----	12 + 4 -----	18 − 6 -----	11 + 3 -----	18 − 7 -----
17 − 3 -----	14 + 3 -----	17 − 4 -----	10 + 4 -----	19 − 2 -----

8.1a. Mixed addition and subtraction in ones place, page 1

Name: _____

17	11	18	16	19
- 7	+ 5	- 8	+ 3	- 5
-----	-----	-----	-----	-----
18	10	17	15	17
- 7	+ 6	- 5	+ 4	- 6
-----	-----	-----	-----	-----
17	15	19	14	18
- 3	+ 2	- 4	+ 3	- 1
-----	-----	-----	-----	-----
17	14	18	13	17
- 1	+ 3	- 3	+ 5	- 2
-----	-----	-----	-----	-----
18	13	19	12	18
- 4	+ 4	- 0	+ 5	- 2
-----	-----	-----	-----	-----

8.1b. Mixed addition and subtraction in ones place, page 2

 More Math, Please! Numbers over 10, © 2002 Zephyr Press, Tucson, AZ • 800-232-2187 • www.zephyrpress.com

Name: _____

11	17	16	16	14
- 1	+ 1	- 5	+ 2	- 4
-----	-----	-----	-----	-----

13	17	11	15	14
- 3	+ 1	- 0	+ 3	- 3
-----	-----	-----	-----	-----

14	16	15	14	12
- 1	+ 1	- 2	+ 4	- 1
-----	-----	-----	-----	-----

16	15	15	13	14
- 4	+ 1	- 3	+ 3	- 4
-----	-----	-----	-----	-----

15	14	16	12	13
- 4	+ 1	- 2	+ 6	- 0
-----	-----	-----	-----	-----

8.1c. Mixed addition and subtraction in ones place, page 3

Name: _____

11 + 7 -----	19 - 1 -----	13 + 6 -----	19 - 7 -----	14 + 2 -----
10 + 8 -----	19 - 3 -----	12 + 5 -----	12 - 2 -----	13 + 3 -----
17 + 2 -----	18 - 5 -----	12 + 6 -----	16 - 5 -----	13 + 5 -----
16 + 3 -----	19 - 7 -----	13 + 6 -----	19 - 4 -----	14 + 4 -----
15 + 4 -----	19 - 8 -----	17 + 2 -----	18 - 4 -----	13 + 2 -----

8.1d. Mixed addition and subtraction in ones place, page 4

More Math, Please! Numbers over 10, © 2002 Zephyr Press, Tucson, AZ • 800-232-2187 • www.zephyrpress.com

Name: _____

12	16	12	19	14
+ 3	- 3	+ 5	- 2	+ 1
-----	-----	-----	-----	-----
11	15	10	18	13
+ 4	- 4	+ 2	- 6	+ 2
-----	-----	-----	-----	-----
10	14	12	17	10
+ 5	- 3	+ 1	- 4	+ 7
-----	-----	-----	-----	-----
13	17	11	19	15
+ 3	- 5	+ 2	- 6	+ 3
-----	-----	-----	-----	-----
12	18	10	19	12
+ 4	- 3	+ 3	- 9	+ 6
-----	-----	-----	-----	-----

8.1e. Mixed addition and subtraction in ones place, page 5

Name: _____

13 + 6 -----	12 - 2 -----	13 + 1 -----	15 - 1 -----	11 + 7 -----
12 + 7 -----	13 - 1 -----	12 + 1 -----	14 - 2 -----	10 + 8 -----
11 + 8 -----	14 - 2 -----	11 + 6 -----	13 - 2 -----	13 + 6 -----
10 + 9 -----	13 - 0 -----	10 + 7 -----	16 - 6 -----	14 + 5 -----
18 + 1 -----	15 - 5 -----	17 + 1 -----	16 - 3 -----	13 + 2 -----

8.1f. Mixed addition and subtraction in ones place, page 6

More Math, Please! Numbers over 10, © 2002 Zephyr Press, Tucson, AZ • 800-232-2187 • www.zephyrpress.com

Name: _____

15	8	11	9	14
- 9	+ 9	- 9	+ 7	- 9
-----	-----	-----	-----	-----
18	9	18	6	16
- 9	+ 2	- 9	+ 9	- 9
-----	-----	-----	-----	-----
12	7	15	9	17
- 9	+ 9	- 9	+ 4	- 9
-----	-----	-----	-----	----
16	9	13	9	18
- 9	+ 6	- 9	+ 3	- 9
-----	-----	-----	-----	-----
11	6	12	9	15
- 9	+ 9	- 9	+ 7	- 9
-----	-----	-----	-----	-----

8.2a. Mixed addition and subtraction of nines, page 1

Name: _____

9 + 2 -----	14 - 9 -----	12 - 9 -----	4 + 9 -----	9 + 9 -----
3 + 9 -----	16 - 9 -----	13 - 9 -----	9 + 3 -----	5 + 9 -----
9 + 8 -----	17 - 9 ----	11 - 9 -----	9 + 6 -----	9 + 5 -----
9 + 2 -----	18 - 9 -----	14 - 9 -----	5 + 9 -----	9 + 9 -----
4 + 9 -----	15 - 9 -----	16 - 9 -----	9 + 3 -----	9 + 5 -----

8.2b. Mixed addition and subtraction of nines, page 2

More Math, Please! Numbers over 10, © 2002 Zephyr Press, Tucson, AZ • 800-232-2187 • www.zephyrpress.com

Name: _____

14 - 8 -----	5 + 8 -----	12 - 8 -----	4 + 8 -----	15 - 8 -----
16 - 8 -----	8 + 9 -----	13 - 8 -----	3 + 8 -----	17 - 8 -----
15 - 8 ----	8 + 7 -----	11 - 8 -----	8 + 4 -----	12 - 8 -----
18 - 8 -----	8 + 6 -----	14 - 8 -----	5 + 8 -----	16 - 8 -----
15 - 8 -----	8 + 5 -----	16 - 8 -----	8 + 3 -----	11 - 8 -----

8.3a. Mixed addition and subtraction of eights, page 1

Name: _____

13 - 8 -----	11 - 8 -----	8 + 6 -----	14 - 8 -----	8 + 7 -----
17 - 8 -----	18 - 8 -----	8 + 9 -----	16 - 8 -----	3 + 8 -----
14 - 8 -----	15 - 8 -----	8 + 7 -----	17 - 8 ----	8 + 6 -----
12 - 8 -----	13 - 8 -----	8 + 6 -----	15 - 8 -----	8 + 3 -----
16 - 8 -----	11 - 8 -----	8 + 5 -----	16 - 8 ------	8 + 4 -----

8.3b. Mixed addition and subtraction of eights, page 2

Name: _____

8	14	12	15	6
+ 7	- 7	- 7	- 7	+ 7
-----	-----	-----	-----	-----

8	16	13	7	18
+ 7	- 7	- 7	+ 7	- 7
-----	-----	-----	-----	-----

4	17	11	6	12
+ 7	- 7	- 7	+ 7	- 7
-----	----	-----	-----	-----

13	18	9	7	19
- 7	- 7	+ 7	+ 7	- 7
-----	-----	-----	-----	-----

12	9	5	8	11
- 7	+ 7	+ 7	+ 7	- 7
-----	-----	-----	-----	-----

8.4a. Mixed addition and subtraction of sevens, page 1

Name: _____

6 + 7 -----	14 - 7 -----	12 - 7 -----	8 + 7 -----	15 - 7 -----
18 - 7 -----	16 - 7 -----	13 - 7 -----	8 + 7 -----	7 + 7 -----
12 - 7 -----	17 - 7 ----	11 - 7 -----	4 + 7 -----	6 + 7 -----
19 - 7 -----	18 - 7 -----	9 + 7 -----	13 - 7 -----	7 + 7 -----
11 - 7 -----	9 + 7 -----	5 + 7 -----	12 - 7 -----	8 + 7 -----

8.4b. Mixed addition and subtraction of sevens, page 2

More Math, Please! Numbers over 10, © 2002 Zephyr Press, Tucson, AZ • 800-232-2187 • www.zephyrpress.com

Name: _____

11 - 6 -----	14 - 6 -----	12 - 6 -----	15 - 6 -----
5 + 6 -----	9 + 6 -----	13 - 6 -----	18 - 6 -----
7 + 6 -----	17 - 6 ----	6 + 6 -----	8 + 6 -----
15 - 6 -----	12 - 6 -----	14 - 6 -----	9 + 6 -----
7 + 6 -----	15 - 6 -----	6 + 6 -----	5 + 6 -----

8.5a. Mixed addition and subtraction of sixes, page 1

Name: _____

12	15	11	14	12
- 6	- 6	- 6	- 6	- 6
-----	-----	-----	-----	-----

13	18	5	9	15
- 6	- 6	+ 6	+ 6	- 6
-----	-----	-----	-----	-----

6	8	7	17	13
+ 6	+ 6	+ 6	- 6	- 6
-----	-----	-----	-----	-----

14	9	15	12	14
- 6	+ 6	- 6	- 6	- 6
-----	-----	-----	-----	-----

6	5	7	15	11
+ 6	+ 6	+ 6	- 6	- 6
-----	-----	-----	-----	-----

8.5b. Mixed addition and subtraction of sixes, page 2

 More Math, Please! Numbers over 10, © 2002 Zephyr Press, Tucson, AZ • 800-232-2187 • www.zephyrpress.com

Name: _____

8 +7 -----	15 - 7 -----	9 + 7 -----	14 - 8 -----	4 + 8 -----
7 + 9 -----	18 - 7 -----	8 + 8 -----	16 - 8 -----	3 + 8 -----
6 + 5 -----	12 - 7 -----	9 + 6 -----	17 - 8 ----	7 + 4 -----
7 + 6 -----	19 - 7 -----	9 + 3 -----	18 - 8 -----	5 + 7 -----
6 + 9 -----	11 - 7 -----	9 + 4 -----	15 - 8 -----	7 + 6 -----

8.6a. Mixed addition and subtraction, sixes–nines, page 1

Name: _____

15 - 7 -----	9 + 2 -----	11 - 8 -----	8 + 7 -----	11 - 9 -----
18 - 7 -----	9 + 3 -----	18 - 8 -----	7 + 9 -----	18 - 9 -----
12 - 7 -----	4 + 9 -----	15 - 8 -----	6 + 5 -----	15 - 9 -----
19 - 7 -----	9 + 5 -----	13 - 8 -----	7 + 6 -----	13 - 9 -----
11 - 7 -----	6 + 9 -----	12 - 8 -----	6 + 6 -----	12 - 9 -----

8.6b. Mixed addition and subtraction, sixes–nines, page 2

 More Math, Please! Numbers over 10, © 2002 Zephyr Press, Tucson, AZ • 800-232-2187 • www.zephyrpress.com

Name: _____

14 - 9 -----	9 + 9 -----	14 - 8 -----	9 + 2 -----	14 - 7 -----
16 - 9 -----	8 + 9 -----	16 - 8 -----	7 + 6 -----	16 - 7 -----
17 - 9 -----	9 + 7 -----	17 - 8 -----	4 + 9 -----	17 - 7 -----
18 - 9 -----	8 + 4 -----	14 - 6 -----	6 + 5 -----	13 - 6 -----
15 - 6 -----	8 + 5 -----	15 - 8 -----	6 + 9 -----	15 - 7 -----

8.6c. Mixed addition and subtraction, sixes–nines, page 3

Name: _____

8 + 3 -----	14 - 5 -----	4 + 8 -----	12 - 5 -----	13 - 4 -----
2 + 9 -----	11 - 4 -----	3 + 8 -----	13 - 4 -----	12 - 4 -----
9 + 4 -----	12 - 3 -----	7 + 4 -----	11 - 3 -----	12 - 5 -----
9 + 3 -----	14 - 5 -----	5 + 7 -----	13 - 5 -----	12 - 5 -----
7 + 5 -----	13 - 4 -----	5 + 6 -----	12 - 4 -----	11 - 4 -----

8.7a. Mixed addition and subtraction, twos–fives, page 1

 More Math, Please! Numbers over 10, © 2002 Zephyr Press, Tucson, AZ • 800-232-2187 • www.zephyrpress.com

Name: _____

12	12	13	8	14
- 5	- 3	- 4	+ 3	- 5
-----	-----	-----	-----	-----
13	13	12	2	11
- 4	- 5	- 4	+ 9	- 4
-----	-----	-----	-----	-----
11	11	12	9	12
- 3	- 4	- 3	+ 4	- 3
-----	-----	-----	-----	-----
14	11	12	9	14
- 5	- 3	- 5	+ 3	- 5
-----	-----	-----	-----	-----
12	13	11	7	13
- 3	- 5	- 4	+ 5	- 4
-----	-----	-----	-----	-----

8.7b. Mixed addition and subtraction, twos–fives, page 2

Name: _____

9	19	4	16	12
+ 2	+ 1	+ 8	+ 2	+ 7
-----	-----	-----	-----	-----
3	17	3	15	13
+ 9	+ 1	+ 8	+ 3	+ 7
-----	-----	-----	-----	-----
9	16	8	14	11
+ 8	+ 1	+ 4	+ 4	+ 7
-----	-----	-----	-----	-----
9	15	5	13	9
+ 2	+ 1	+ 8	+ 3	+ 7
-----	-----	-----	-----	-----
4	14	8	12	5
+ 9	+ 1	+ 3	+ 6	+ 7
-----	-----	-----	-----	-----

8.8a. Mixed addition practice, page 1

More Math, Please! Numbers over 10, © 2002 Zephyr Press, Tucson, AZ • 800-232-2187 • www.zephyrpress.com

Name: _____

9 + 9 -----	19 + 1 -----	9 + 7 -----	13 + 1 -----	4 + 8 -----
8 + 9 -----	12 + 6 -----	8 + 8 -----	14 + 2 -----	3 + 8 -----
9 + 7 -----	16 + 3 -----	9 + 6 -----	15 + 3 -----	7 + 4 -----
8 + 4 -----	12 + 4 -----	9 + 3 -----	11 + 3 -----	5 + 7 -----
8 + 5 -----	14 + 3 -----	9 + 4 -----	10 + 4 -----	7 + 6 -----

8.8b. Mixed addition practice, page 2

Name: _____

12 - 6 -----	19 - 5 -----	14 - 9 -----	13 - 2 -----	12 - 8 -----
15 - 6 -----	17 - 6 -----	16 - 9 -----	15 - 3 -----	13 - 8 -----
13 - 6 -----	18 - 1 -----	17 - 9 -----	19 - 6 -----	11 - 8 -----
14 - 6 -----	17 - 2 -----	18 - 9 -----	18 - 6 -----	14 - 8 -----
11 - 6 -----	18 - 2 -----	15 - 9 -----	17 - 4 -----	16 - 8 -----

8.9a. Mixed subtraction practice, page 1

More Math, Please! Numbers over 10, © 2002 Zephyr Press, Tucson, AZ • 800-232-2187 • www.zephyrpress.com

Name: _____

11	16	14	15	18
- 1	- 7	- 2	- 9	- 8
-----	-----	-----	-----	-----

18	18	13	18	17
- 5	- 7	- 3	- 9	- 5
-----	-----	-----	-----	-----

17	12	18	12	19
- 2	- 7	- 6	- 9	- 4
-----	-----	-----	-----	-----

16	19	18	16	18
- 5	- 7	- 7	- 9	- 3
-----	-----	-----	-----	-----

17	11	19	11	19
- 3	- 7	- 2	- 9	- 0
-----	-----	-----	-----	-----

8.9b. Mixed subtraction practice, page 2

Name: _____

11 - 1 -----	12 + 7 -----	13 - 6 -----	13 + 8 -----	14 - 2 -----
13 + 5 -----	12 - 6 -----	15 + 7 -----	14 - 2 -----	13 + 3 -----
17 - 9 -----	16 + 6 -----	19 - 6 -----	15 + 3 -----	18 - 9 -----
16 + 7 -----	16 - 4 -----	13 + 6 -----	11 - 3 -----	12 + 7 -----
17 - 8 -----	14 + 8 -----	17 - 4 -----	10 + 4 -----	15 - 8 -----

8.10a. Mixed addition and subtraction practice, page 1

More Math, Please! Numbers over 10, © 2002 Zephyr Press, Tucson, AZ • 800-232-2187 • www.zephyrpress.com

Name: _____

14 - 1 -----	13 + 5 -----	14 - 6 -----	13 + 6 -----	17 - 2 -----
14 + 5 -----	15 - 8 -----	12 + 7 -----	17 - 2 -----	16 + 3 -----
15 - 9 -----	18 + 6 -----	18 - 6 -----	14 + 3 -----	16 - 9 -----
14 + 7 -----	17 - 4 -----	12 + 6 -----	14 - 6 -----	11 + 7 -----
15 - 8 -----	16 + 8 -----	19 - 4 -----	12 + 4 -----	16 - 8 -----

8.10b. Mixed addition and subtraction practice, page 2

Name: _____

44	53	45	64	54
- 22	+ 21	- 24	+ 13	- 32
-----	-----	-----	-----	-----
13	47	55	54	13
+ 25	- 26	+ 24	- 32	+ 33
-----	-----	-----	-----	-----
37	16	59	15	88
- 26	+ 42	- 36	+ 83	- 33
-----	-----	-----	-----	-----
12	46	13	66	62
+ 47	- 24	+ 46	- 33	+ 37
-----	-----	-----	-----	-----
87	84	77	23	75
- 35	+ 15	- 44	+ 46	- 53
-----	-----	-----	-----	-----

9.1a. Basic multi-digit addition and subtraction, page 1

 More Math, Please! Numbers over 10, © 2002 Zephyr Press, Tucson, AZ • 800-232-2187 • www.zephyrpress.com

Name: _____

53	35	75	54	84
- 23	+ 21	- 24	+ 15	- 72
-----	-----	-----	-----	-----
43	67	45	78	33
+ 24	- 46	+ 23	- 37	+ 33
-----	-----	-----	-----	-----
57	36	49	45	83
- 24	+ 41	- 36	+ 43	- 52
-----	-----	-----	-----	-----
52	48	33	64	54
+ 47	- 26	+ 46	- 32	+ 35
-----	-----	-----	-----	-----
99	88	77	66	55
- 35	- 15	- 44	+ 23	- 53
-----	-----	-----	-----	-----

9.1b. Basic multi-digit addition and subtraction, page 2

Name: _____

434	523	465	654	584
- 222	+ 221	- 234	+ 123	- 352
------	------	------	------	------

143	467	152	564	173
+ 245	- 246	+ 237	- 332	+ 313
------	------	------	------	------

387	136	589	146	848
- 256	+ 442	- 366	+ 853	- 333
------	------	------	------	------

222	476	163	656	642
+ 437	- 254	+ 436	- 333	+ 357
------	------	------	------	------

87	84	77	23	75
- 35	+ 15	- 44	+ 46	- 53
------	------	------	------	------

9.1c. Basic multi-digit addition and subtraction, page 3

Name: _____

4534	5333	4765	6554
- 2422	+ 2524	- 2544	+ 3245
-------	-------	-------	-------

5343	4867	5325	5984
+ 2535	- 2756	+ 2344	- 3652
-------	--------	-------	-------

36667	23246	55649	23425
- 24436	+ 42532	- 33326	+ 63373
--------	--------	--------	--------

32432	43646	25433	67876
+ 42357	- 22334	+ 44246	- 35653
-------	--------	--------	---------

886567	7234324	778887	24323
- 323225	+ 2523225	- 455554	+ 42346
----------	-----------	----------	---------

9.1d. Basic multi-digit addition and subtraction, page 4

Name: _____

```
  4 4 5 6 8 6 7 5 4 6 7 8 9 4
- 2 3 2 4 3 2 2 4 3 3 4 5 6 2
---------------------------------
```

```
  7 4 6 7 3 4 3 2 6 4 5 3 6 2 4 3 3
+ 2 3 2 2 5 3 2 5 2 4 4 3 2 3 2 3 5
-------------------------------------
```

```
  3 9 7 8 6 9 8 7 8 9 7 6 8 7 9 7 8 9 7 8 7 6 8 9 7
- 2 4 2 4 3 5 2 4 3 3 2 3 2 2 3 4 5 3 4 2 3 4 2 4 6
-----------------------------------------------------
```

```
  1 5 3 4 5 4 3 3 2 2 4 3 4 5 2
+ 1 3 2 4 4 3 3 2 5 4 5 4 3 2 4
---------------------------------
```

```
  8 5 3 5 4 4 7 8 9 4 5 7
- 3 0 2 3 2 3 3 4 3 2 2 5
---------------------------
```

9.1e. Basic multi-digit addition and subtraction, page 5

Name: _____

Name: _____

14 + 17 ------	13 + 18 ------
18 + 25 ------	27 + 26 ------
17 + 16 ------	16 + 47 ------
19 + 47 ------	16 + 27 ------
28 + 35 ------	77 + 15 ------

14 + 19 ------	14 + 18 ------
29 + 29 ------	18 + 27 ------
15 + 29 ------	18 + 37 ------
26 + 28 ------	24 + 37 ------
23 + 48 ------	35 + 58 ------

9.2a. Double-digit make a ten, page 1

9.2a. Double-digit make a ten, page 2

Name: _____

34 + 57 - - - - -	23 + 48 - - - - -
68 + 25 - - - - -	57 + 27 - - - - -
37 + 36 - - - - -	46 + 27 - - - - -
49 + 47 - - - - -	56 + 24 - - - - -
68 + 24 - - - - -	66 + 25 - - - - -

9.2b. Double-digit make a ten, page 3

Name: _____

34 + 49 - - - - -	34 + 28 - - - - -
29 + 67 - - - - -	48 + 26 - - - - -
75 + 19 - - - - -	68 + 35 - - - - -
46 + 25 - - - - -	46 + 37 - - - - -
34 + 48 - - - - -	37 + 48 - - - - -

9.2b. Double-digit make a ten, page 4

More Math, Please! Numbers over 10, © 2002 Zephyr Press, Tucson, AZ • 800-232-2187 • www.zephyrpress.com

Name: _____

23 + 37 -----	46 + 28 -----
48 + 25 -----	47 + 26 -----
37 + 46 -----	46 + 47 -----
49 + 47 -----	36 + 28 -----
59 + 35 -----	68 + 25 -----

9.2c. Double-digit make a ten, page 5

Name: _____

45 + 29 -----	54 + 38 -----
59 + 28 -----	38 + 47 -----
45 + 29 -----	58 + 37 -----
56 + 29 -----	44 + 38 -----
53 + 39 -----	35 + 57 -----

9.2c. Double-digit make a ten, page 6

Name: _____

34	63
- 7	- 8
-----	-----

78	53
- 9	- 6
-----	-----

77	86
- 8	- 9
-----	-----

52	46
- 7	- 7
-----	-----

92	77
- 7	- 8
-----	-----

9.3. Single-digit take from ten, page 1

Name: _____

94	74
- 9	- 8
-----	-----

81	32
- 9	- 6
-----	-----

55	84
- 9	- 7
-----	-----

66	54
- 8	- 7
-----	-----

63	75
- 8	- 8
-----	-----

9.3. Single-digit take from ten, page 2

 More Math, Please! Numbers over 10, © 2002 Zephyr Press, Tucson, AZ • 800-232-2187 • www.zephyrpress.com

Name: _____

44 − 22 -----	14 + 17 -----
13 + 25 -----	18 + 25 -----
37 − 26 -----	17 + 16 -----
12 + 47 -----	19 + 47 -----
87 − 35 -----	28 + 35 -----

9.4. Mixed problems, page 1

Name: _____

523 + 221 -------	63 − 8 -----
467 − 246 -------	53 − 6 -----
136 + 442 -------	86 − 9 -----
476 − 254 -------	46 − 7 -----
84 + 15 -------	77 − 8 -----

9.4. Mixed problems, page 2

Name: _____

Name: _____

$$\begin{array}{r} 34 \\ -\ 27 \\ \hline \end{array}$$

$$\begin{array}{r} 63 \\ -\ 28 \\ \hline \end{array}$$

$$\begin{array}{r} 84 \\ -\ 39 \\ \hline \end{array}$$

$$\begin{array}{r} 74 \\ -\ 38 \\ \hline \end{array}$$

$$\begin{array}{r} 78 \\ -\ 29 \\ \hline \end{array}$$

$$\begin{array}{r} 53 \\ -\ 26 \\ \hline \end{array}$$

$$\begin{array}{r} 82 \\ -\ 29 \\ \hline \end{array}$$

$$\begin{array}{r} 32 \\ -\ 26 \\ \hline \end{array}$$

$$\begin{array}{r} 77 \\ -\ 28 \\ \hline \end{array}$$

$$\begin{array}{r} 86 \\ -\ 27 \\ \hline \end{array}$$

$$\begin{array}{r} 55 \\ -\ 29 \\ \hline \end{array}$$

$$\begin{array}{r} 84 \\ -\ 37 \\ \hline \end{array}$$

$$\begin{array}{r} 52 \\ -\ 35 \\ \hline \end{array}$$

$$\begin{array}{r} 46 \\ -\ 37 \\ \hline \end{array}$$

$$\begin{array}{r} 66 \\ -\ 28 \\ \hline \end{array}$$

$$\begin{array}{r} 54 \\ -\ 27 \\ \hline \end{array}$$

$$\begin{array}{r} 92 \\ -\ 46 \\ \hline \end{array}$$

$$\begin{array}{r} 77 \\ -\ 28 \\ \hline \end{array}$$

$$\begin{array}{r} 63 \\ -\ 28 \\ \hline \end{array}$$

$$\begin{array}{r} 75 \\ -\ 28 \\ \hline \end{array}$$

9.5. Double-digit take from ten, page 1

9.5. Double-digit take from ten, page 2

Name: _____

$$\begin{array}{r} 94 \\ -\ 9 \\ \hline \end{array} \qquad \begin{array}{r} 23 \\ +\ 48 \\ \hline \end{array}$$

$$\begin{array}{r} 81 \\ -\ 9 \\ \hline \end{array} \qquad \begin{array}{r} 57 \\ +\ 27 \\ \hline \end{array}$$

$$\begin{array}{r} 55 \\ -\ 9 \\ \hline \end{array} \qquad \begin{array}{r} 46 \\ +\ 27 \\ \hline \end{array}$$

$$\begin{array}{r} 66 \\ -\ 8 \\ \hline \end{array} \qquad \begin{array}{r} 56 \\ +\ 24 \\ \hline \end{array}$$

$$\begin{array}{r} 63 \\ -\ 8 \\ \hline \end{array} \qquad \begin{array}{r} 66 \\ +\ 25 \\ \hline \end{array}$$

9.6. Mixed problems for assessment, page 1

Name: _____

$$\begin{array}{r} 74 \\ -\ 38 \\ \hline \end{array} \qquad \begin{array}{r} 45 \\ +\ 29 \\ \hline \end{array}$$

$$\begin{array}{r} 32 \\ -\ 26 \\ \hline \end{array} \qquad \begin{array}{r} 59 \\ +\ 28 \\ \hline \end{array}$$

$$\begin{array}{r} 84 \\ -\ 37 \\ \hline \end{array} \qquad \begin{array}{r} 45 \\ +\ 29 \\ \hline \end{array}$$

$$\begin{array}{r} 54 \\ -\ 27 \\ \hline \end{array} \qquad \begin{array}{r} 56 \\ +\ 29 \\ \hline \end{array}$$

$$\begin{array}{r} 75 \\ -\ 28 \\ \hline \end{array} \qquad \begin{array}{r} 53 \\ +\ 49 \\ \hline \end{array}$$

9.6. Mixed problems for assessment, page 2

Name: _____

$$134 + 177$$

$$173 + 178$$

$$168 + 275$$

$$267 + 275$$

$$167 + 156$$

$$156 + 477$$

$$159 + 457$$

$$166 + 267$$

$$28 + 35$$

$$77 + 15$$

9.7. Multi-digit make a ten, page 1

Name: _____

$$184 + 189$$

$$154 + 178$$

$$279 + 269$$

$$188 + 267$$

$$135 + 299$$

$$148 + 377$$

$$296 + 248$$

$$284 + 357$$

$$283 + 478$$

$$365 + 588$$

9.7. Multi-digit make a ten, page 2

More Math, Please! Numbers over 10, © 2002 Zephyr Press, Tucson, AZ • 800-232-2187 • www.zephyrpress.com

Name: _____

Name: _____

364 - 177 -------	623 - 178 -------	844 - 359 -------	744 - 368 -------
748 - 169 -------	533 - 166 -------	831 - 279 -------	322 - 276 -------
737 - 168 -------	846 - 179 -------	535 - 269 -------	844 - 367 -------
542 - 177 -------	466 - 187 -------	626 - 248 -------	534 - 267 -------
932 - 167 -------	747 - 178 -------	643 - 288 -------	745 - 278 -------

9.8. Multi-digit take from ten, page 1

9.8. Multi-digit take from ten, page 2

Appendix B
Tracking Charts and Progress Reports

Individual Assessment: **Computation to Ten** (Chapter 2)

Name _____

Based on several observations and samples of written work, draw a line through each problem as it is mastered. When an entire street has been mastered, enter the date of mastery. Note any needs for additional practice in the last column.

Street	Date of Mastery	Extra Practice Needed
Third: 0 + 3 1 + 2		
Fourth: 0 + 4 1 + 3 2 + 2		
Fifth: 0 + 5 1 + 4 2 + 3		
Sixth: 0 + 6 1 + 5 2 + 4 3 + 3		
Seventh: 0 + 7 1 + 6 2 + 5 3 + 4		
Eighth: 0 + 8 1 + 7 2 + 6 3 + 5 4 + 4		
Ninth: 0 + 9 1 + 8 2 + 7 3 + 6 4 + 5		
Tenth: 0 + 10 1 + 9 2 + 8 3 + 7 4 + 6 5 + 5		

Individual Assessment: **Computation to Ten** (Chapter 2)

Name _____

Based on several observations and samples of written work, draw a line through each problem as it is mastered. When an entire street has been mastered, enter the date of mastery. Note any needs for additional practice in the last column.

Street	Date of Mastery	Extra Practice Needed
Third: 0 + 3 1 + 2		
Fourth: 0 + 4 1 + 3 2 + 2		
Fifth: 0 + 5 1 + 4 2 + 3		
Sixth: 0 + 6 1 + 5 2 + 4 3 + 3		
Seventh: 0 + 7 1 + 6 2 + 5 3 + 4		
Eighth: 0 + 8 1 + 7 2 + 6 3 + 5 4 + 4		
Ninth: 0 + 9 1 + 8 2 + 7 3 + 6 4 + 5		
Tenth: 0 + 10 1 + 9 2 + 8 3 + 7 4 + 6 5 + 5		

Whole-Class Record (Chapter 2)

Check off each street when student shows mastery

Name	Third	Fourth	Fifth	Sixth	Seventh	Eighth	Ninth	Tenth

More Math, Please! Numbers over 10, © 2002 Zephyr Press, Tucson, AZ • 800-232-2187 • www.zephyrpress.com

Whole-Class Record (Chapter 2)

Check off each skill when student shows mastery

Name	Dot Cards	Fives Frames to 20	Fives Frames to 70	My Two Hands	Houses

Whole-Class Record (Chapters 3–4)

Check off each skill as the student demonstrates mastery

Name	Keeps the correct number of sticks in ones and tens places	Makes a ten and places correctly on mat	Takes from ten and places remaining ones correctly	Subtracts from ones place before tens place	Is fluent with method and procedures

Place Value

Progress Report (Chapters 3–4)

Name _____   Date _____

Constructing:	child is still working through the procedure	
Emerging:	child uses the correct procedure but is hesitant	
Fluent:	child can use the procedure confidently	

	Constructing	Emerging	Fluent	Comments:
Keeps the correct number of sticks in ones and tens places				
Makes a ten and places correctly on mat				
Takes from ten and places remaining ones correctly				
Subtracts from ones place before tens place				
Is fluent with method and procedures				

✂ - ✂

Place Value

Progress Report (Chapters 3–4)

Name _____   Date _____

Constructing:	child is still working through the procedure	
Emerging:	child uses the correct procedure but is hesitant	
Fluent:	child can use the procedure confidently	

	Constructing	Emerging	Fluent	Comments:
Keeps the correct number of sticks in ones and tens places				
Makes a ten and places correctly on mat				
Takes from ten and places remaining ones correctly				
Subtracts from ones place before tens place				
Is fluent with method and procedures				

Whole-Class Record (Chapters 5–7)

Check off each skill as the student demonstrates mastery

Name	Adds ones	Subtracts ones	Makes a ten (adding)	Takes from ten (subtracting)	Tells a story demonstrating understanding of symbols

More Math, Please! Numbers over 10, © 2002 Zephyr Press, Tucson, AZ • 800-232-2187 • www.zephyrpress.com

Computation

Progress Report (Chapters 5–7)

Name _____ Date _____

Constructing:	child is still working through the procedure
Emerging:	child uses the correct procedure but is hesitant
Fluent:	child can use the procedure confidently

	Constructing	Emerging	Fluent	Comments:
Adds ones				
Subtracts ones				
Makes a ten (adding)				
Takes from ten (subtracting)				
Tells a story demonstrating understanding of symbols				

✂ - ✂

Computation

Progress Report (Chapters 5–7)

Name _____ Date _____

Constructing:	child is still working through the procedure
Emerging:	child uses the correct procedure but is hesitant
Fluent:	child can use the procedure confidently

	Constructing	Emerging	Fluent	Comments:
Adds ones				
Subtracts ones				
Makes a ten (adding)				
Takes from ten (subtracting)				
Tells a story demonstrating understanding of symbols				

Whole-Class Record (Chapters 8–9)

Check off each skill as the student demonstrates mastery

Name	Tells a story matching the three parts of a problem	Adds and subtracts ones in multi-digit numbers	Makes a ten with double-digit numbers	Takes from ten with double-digit numbers	Makes a ten and takes from ten with multi-digit numbers

More Math, Please! Numbers over 10, © 2002 Zephyr Press, Tucson, AZ • 800-232-2187 • www.zephyrpress.com

Progress Report (Chapters 8–9)

To the Top!

Name _____   Date _____

	Constructing: child is still working through the procedure Emerging: child uses the correct procedure but is hesitant Fluent: child can use the procedure confidently

	Constructing	Emerging	Fluent	Comments:
Tells a story matching the three parts of a problem				
Adds and subtracts ones in multi-digit numbers				
Makes a ten with double-digit numbers				
Takes from ten with double-digit numbers				
Makes a ten and takes from ten with multi-digit numbers				

✂ -- ✂

Progress Report (Chapters 8–9)

To the Top!

Name _____   Date _____

	Constructing: child is still working through the procedure Emerging: child uses the correct procedure but is hesitant Fluent: child can use the procedure confidently

	Constructing	Emerging	Fluent	Comments:
Tells a story matching the three parts of a problem				
Adds and subtracts ones in multi-digit numbers				
Makes a ten with double-digit numbers				
Takes from ten with double-digit numbers				
Makes a ten and takes from ten with multi-digit numbers				

References

Barbe, Walter B. 1985. *Growing Up Learning*. Washington, D.C.: Acropolis Books.

Caine, Geoffrey, Renate Nummela Caine, and Sam Crowell. 1999. *MindShifts: A Brain-Compatible Process for Professional Growth and the Renewal of Education*. Rev. ed. Tucson, Ariz.: Zephyr Press.

Gardner, Howard. 1993. *Frames of Mind: The Theory of Multiple Intelligences*. 2nd. ed. New York: Harper and Row.

Gregorc, Anthony F. 1982. *An Adult's Guide to Style*. Columbia, Conn.: Gregorc Associates. (Available from 5 Doubleday Rd., Columbia, Conn. 06237. (203) 228-0093.)

Hart, Leslie. 1999. *Human Brain and Human Learning*. Kent, Wash.: Books for Educators.

Jensen, Eric. 1994. *The Learning Brain*. Del Mar, Calif.: Turning Point.

————. 1998. *Teaching with the Brain in Mind*. Alexandria, Va.: ASCD.

LeDoux, Joseph. 1996. *The Emotional Brain: The Mysterious Underpinnings of Emotional Life*. New York: Simon and Schuster.

Swassing, Raymond, and Walter Barbe. 1999. Swassing-Barbe Modality Index. In *Modality Kit*. Columbus, OH: Zaner-Bloser, Inc.

Tobias, Cynthia Ulrich. 1994. *The Way They Learn*. Colorado Springs, Colo.: Focus on the Family Publishing.

Witkin, Herman A. 1977. Cognitive Styles in the Educational Setting. *New York University Education Quarterly*, 14–20.

Index

Note: Page numbers in **bold** refer to Reproducible Blackline Masters

About the Author

Sarah Morgan does extensive Title 1 teaching with grades PreK through third in a public school. She is a fluent Spanish speaker and is the primary ESOL (English for Speakers of Other Languages) instructor in her school where she is able to use the innovative reading program she has developed. In addition, Sarah provides training, materials, and support to classroom teachers to help them meet learners' needs within the regular classroom. She holds a B.A. in art from Wheaton College, Wheaton, Illinois; and an M.Ed. from Aquinas College in Grand Rapids, Michigan. Her passion and expertise are in providing learning tools and teacher support in order to enable struggling students to excel in their regular classrooms. During her years of working with students who struggle in math and reading, Sarah developed a reading method that is now being used within three Michigan school districts in regular and special education classrooms. She has also developed a three-book series, *More Math, Please!*, that progresses from learning numbers to multiplication and division. The materials and methods are rich in visual and kinesthetic components that make learning quick and effortless for the students. Sarah's passions outside of work include her two artist-musician children, Matthew and Melissa; gardening; beaching it; music; books; and writing.